EXPLORING ENGLAND
BY CANAL

EXPLORING ENGLAND BY CANAL

David Owen

DAVID & CHARLES
Newton Abbot   London   North Pomfret (Vt)

By the same author

CANALS TO MANCHESTER

CHESHIRE WATERWAYS

KIRKSTALL ABBEY

THE MANCHESTER SHIP CANAL

THE STORY OF MERSEY AND DEESIDE ROCKS

WATER BYWAYS

WATER HIGHWAYS

WATER RALLIES

Unless otherwise indicated all the photographs are from the author's collection.

British Library Cataloguing in Publication Data

Owen, David E.
  Exploring England by canal.
  1. Boats and boating – England   2. Canal-boats
  – England
  I. Title
  797.1   GV835.3.G7

  ISBN 0-7153-8768-5

Typeset by Typesetters (Birmingham) Limited
Smethwick, West Midlands
and printed in Great Britain
by Butler & Tanner Limited, Frome and London
for David & Charles Publishers plc
Brunel House   Newton Abbot   Devon

Published in the United States of America
by David & Charles Inc
North Pomfret   Vermont 05053   USA

CONTENTS

INTRODUCTION

Many people are completely unaware of the existence of canals, even when they live quite close to one. To others, the towpath is a good place away from the traffic to take the dog for a walk, but even then they have no idea that the waterway goes more than a few miles in each direction. Before my wife and I discovered canals ourselves, we lived in Leeds and often crossed the Leeds & Liverpool Canal at Apperley Bridge. A few hundred yards to the west and well in view from the bridge is one of the staircase locks, yet we never noticed it. In those days there was still barge traffic but I do not recall seeing a boat moving.

The lock and round-house at Gailey stand beside the A5 main road and, a few miles to the west, the Shropshire Union (or Shroppie) crosses the same road on a beautifully designed aqueduct. Yet the motorist, travelling fast along the straight Holyhead road, notices neither. Rivers have always appeared as things of beauty, except perhaps those unfortunate streams that rush in and out of culverts in our major towns. Canals, to those who do not know and love them, are either weed-grown ditches or rubbish-strewn channels dominated by the gasworks.

The real beauty of the rural navigation is rarely seen as it wanders through fields and woodlands far from the busy roads. Many of the eighteenth- and early nineteenth-century warehouses have disappeared or lie empty and windowless in derelict areas; people are only just beginning to accept that those left are architectural gems. The huge flights of locks are hard to find except by water and the aqueducts and tunnels are seldom by the roadside.

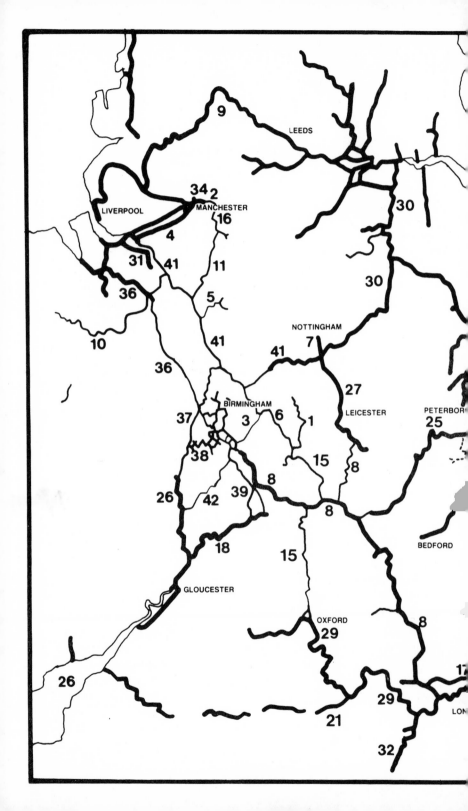

BCN CANALS

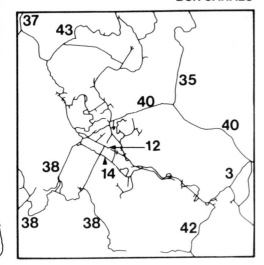

KEY

▬▬▬▬ Wide Canals
───── Narrow Canals
- - - - - Navigable Drains

1 Ashby Canal
2 Ashton Canal
3 Birmingham & Fazeley Canal
4 Bridgewater Canal
5 Caldon Canal
6 Coventry Canal
7 Erewash Canal
8 Grand Union Canal
9 Leeds and Liverpool Canal
10 Llangollen Canal
11 Macclesfield Canal
12 Main Line BCN
13 Middle Level
14 Old Main Line BCN
15 Oxford Canal
16 Peak Forest Canal
17 Regents Canal
18 R. Avon
19 R. Cam & Lodes
20 R. Great Ouse
21 R. Kennet
22 R. Lark
23 R. Lee
24 R. Little Ouse
25 R. Nene
26 R. Severn
27 R. Soar
28 R. Stort
29 R. Thames
30 R. Trent
31 R. Weaver
32 R. Wey
33 R. Wissey
34 Rochdale Canal
35 Rushall Canal
36 Shropshire Union Canal
37 Staffs & Worcester Canal
38 Stourbridge & Dudley Canal
39 Stratford Canal
40 Tame Valley Canal BCN
41 Trent & Mersey Canal
42 Worcester & Birmingham Canal
43 Wyrley & Essington Canal

However, once you get to know about canals as a boater or as a towpath explorer, everything is seen in a different light. Whenever we make a long journey by car, we study the map to note the canals that we shall cross and make small detours to enjoy our picnic lunch or tea beside some waterway. We find when boating that those on the canalside are keen to talk: 'Where can you go from here?'; 'Do you really come from Cheshire and did you come all the way by water?'; 'How long did it take?'. These same questions asked us on the Fen rivers, the Kennet, the Stratford Avon and even in London, show that few people realise how far the canals run and how much of the network is still open to navigation.

The purpose of this book is to answer these and the many other questions frequently asked about one aspect or another of the inland-waterway network. In so doing it is my hope that you will be able to gain extra enjoyment from your cruising holiday.

1

CANALS: THE BACKGROUND

What, then, are the canals really like; where do they go and how do they link up? They are channels of level water which climb hills by means of locks and link up with one another, with rivers or with the sea. In Britain they were mostly built for boats and barges pulled by a horse, a mule or a pair of donkeys. Unlike the early river and Fen navigations, they were all built with towpaths. It is the towpaths which provide such attractive walks, for there are wild flowers along the banks and birds in the hedgerows and the nearness of the water adds to the peace of the scene.

Water supply

Two questions that are always asked are: 'Where does the water come from to keep the canal full?' and 'Why does it not all leak away?' No one asks this question of rivers for the answer is obvious. When rain falls, some of it runs into rivulets and some sinks into the ground to reappear as springs. Even the mighty Thames first appears as a spring at Thames Head.

The situation is quite different with canals for although a few streams may trickle into the waterway, most are carried beneath it in culverts. This is necessary, for streams carry silt which would be deposited immediately in the still waters. Canals cross watersheds with locks at both ends of the summit level and every time a boat goes over the top, it takes two lockfuls of water with it. This water must be replaced and so must any that leaks away or evaporates from the surface. In fact, most canals obtain their water from reservoirs built in the hills at a higher level than the canal. The

11

early canal builders were seldom able to calculate the amount of water that would be needed, for canals became increasingly heavily used and more reservoirs were required. In the case of the Trent & Mersey Canal, its offshoot, the Caldon, became a valuable feeder and the Leek branch was added in 1797 largely to enable Rudyard Lake to be built and linked with the system.

A few canals are river-fed. The Sankey Navigation has the Sankey brook running in and out at several points and the former Grand Junction picks up waters from the Colne in its lower reaches. The Llangollen Canal is entirely river-fed and the Horseshoe Falls at Llantisilio were constructed to keep a sufficient head of water flowing through the feeder channel. More canals might have been expected to have been fed in this way but there was usually opposition from mill owners who feared that the loss of river water would bring their waterwheels to a standstill. As water mills usually predated canals, this was a valid objection.

The mighty tunnel at Standedge on the Huddersfield Narrow Canal runs so deeply beneath the hillside that much of it is below the water table – the level of underground waters within the hill. It varies with the wet and dry seasons but there is always some water flowing out of the tunnel at both ends. In the same way, water gushes out of the walls of Harecastle tunnel on the Trent & Mersey, though the volume is not sufficient to feed the canal's top pound (a pound is the stretch of water between two locks). Nor could it ever have replenished the hundreds of lockfuls lost when the canal was at its busiest. Another source of water is the drainage from coal mines. For instance, the main underground canal at Worsley was constructed as a navigable drainage channel though the Bridgewater Canal required additional supplies. Cobb's engine house at Windmill End, south of the Netherton tunnel, housed a pumping engine which raised water from the mines beneath.

The pumping of water from lower pounds is also undertaken, although this occurs more often on European canals where locks are frequently much larger and the loss of water more serious. Pumps have also been built in England where the canal crosses a large enough river. Examples of pumping-houses are to be seen at Lea Wood between the Cromford Canal and the River Derwent, and at Claverton, built to lift water from the Avon to the Kennet & Avon Canal.

Geology

Canals were built on all types of strata, some completely impervious and some porous. On the boulder clays of the North and the marls and lias clays of the Midlands, there was no need to line the canal since no water will seep away through these beds. In sandstones and limestones and areas affected by faulting – cracks in the sub-surface where the strata have moved – the water may quickly drain away. Here some form of lining was necessary and the material most commonly used in construction and maintenance was puddled clay. It was the cheapest and most handy material and indeed it is still in use today. The puddling of clay is a little like the wedging of clay by the potter before the pot is thrown: he pummels and squeezes it manually or mechanically to remove air bubbles and to make it homogeneous. For the lining of canals the clay was dug and laid aside to weather. It then became friable and broke up; when it was needed water was added and it was shovelled into the deep channel. Men wearing their puddling boots trod it into a coherent mass and a considerable thickness was laid over the bottom and sides. When stone banks were built, puddled clay was packed in behind the stonework to prevent seepage. It was important not to let the clay dry out at any time or deep cracks would occur. Once the water was let in the clay seal would normally remain intact and impervious permanently. During the long dry summer of 1976 lengths of the top pound of the Leicester section of the Grand Union Canal became waterless and there was great concern that the puddle would crack. Fortunately, there was enough mud and silt on top to protect it and no leaks occurred when the canal was rewatered.

History

Rivers and estuaries have been used for navigation from time immemorial since pre-Roman Britons hacked out logs and paddled their dug-out canoes. Examples of these have been dug up all over the country and two good specimens were found deep down in the river gravels when the Manchester Ship Canal was constructed. The first true canals in England were dug by the Romans in the eastern counties: perhaps primarily for drainage but certainly also for navigation. Fossdyke, linking Lincoln on the Witham with the Trent at Torksey, is such a canal and, deepened, is still in use today. The short lodes which join the Cam are said to be of Roman origin. These canals run on one level through low-lying country.

In the Middle Ages, several rivers were made navigable further inland by impounding water behind weirs and making movable gates in the weirs. There were many such 'flash locks' on the Thames and this made it possible for barges to carry goods much further inland. Weirs were also built across rivers to provide a head of water to drive mills and there was constant friction between the millers who needed the water power and the boatmen who dropped the level when they opened the water gate. The more satisfactory pound lock, which is the type that we know today, originated on the Continent. The first example in England was on the Exeter Canal, an artificial cut opened in 1566 to avoid the changing channels of the Exe estuary. It had three such locks, each of which was little more than two flash locks placed so close that each could be opened and closed in turn to pass the boat with a minimum waste of water. The earliest 'pound' locks had guillotine gates at both ends; it was Leonardo da

Vinci who is said to have originated the mitred gates seen on English canals. His own drawings of these lock gates designed for a canal in Milan can be seen in the museum in that city. The early locks were usually placed in the river channel but with improved navigations, lock cuts were made often several miles long to avoid shallow stretches of river.

There is much controversy as to which was the first true canal in England, the Sankey Navigation (St Helens Canal) or the Bridgewater Canal. Arguments for the one or the other are really academic since they were both preceded by the Newry Canal in Northern Ireland. The Sankey Navigation ran entirely independently of the little River Sankey except that the stream was used to feed the canal in a number of places. It was, however, built under an Act to make the stream navigable and was opened in 1757. Six years later, the Bridgewater Canal, built under a true canal Act, was open from Worsley to Manchester. The purpose of both was to convey coal from the mines to the markets and each fulfilled that task admirably for a couple of centuries.

The real extension of canals began shortly after these two were opened. The mill engineer, James Brindley, had already surveyed a line from Stoke-on-Trent to the navigable River Trent at Wilden Ferry in 1758, and in 1761 John Smeaton had suggested its extension westwards. The Grand Cross eventually emerged from this: a single canal, the Trent & Mersey, ran from the navigable reaches of the Trent to the Mersey estuary; the Staffordshire & Worcestershire Canal branched off the Trent & Mersey to run down to the Severn at Bewdley, and later Stourport; a further branch, made up of the Coventry and Oxford Canals, reached to the Thames at Oxford. By 1790 four major ports – Liverpool, Bristol, London and Hull – were linked with the Potteries and the developing Black Country.

At the same time, a route was surveyed across the Pennines from Liverpool to the navigable River Aire in Leeds. The Act of Parliament for the Leeds & Liverpool was obtained in

1770, though the canal was not completed until 1816. Several other rather specialised navigations date from this early period, including the Droitwich Canal, linking that town with the Severn. The main cargoes were salt and coal – fuel to boil the brine – carried in barges and the smaller Severn trows. The Chesterfield Canal was also built at this time to reach the Derbyshire coalfield from the Trent. Where it crossed the fairly level ground of Lincolnshire wide locks were built but the long flights through Worksop and the great tunnel at Norwood were built to the narrow gauge. The Erewash Canal on the Derbyshire–Nottinghamshire border was also built at this period and the River Soar was made navigable to Loughborough. Both were constructed with barge locks and the main cargo was coal.

These early canals took time to achieve commercial success, for wharves and warehouses had yet to be built and boats and boatmen to be found to work them. Canals are crossed by many bridges and the estuary sailing craft had to be adapted as barges, with stepped masts and some method of propulsion. Narrowboats had to be designed for the narrow canals which had towpaths built alongside them. Hanson (see Bibliography) notes that the early steerers were most probably carters and farmers, owners of horses, and used to moving goods by road. On early river navigations, boats unable to sail were hauled by gangs of men known as halers but horse towing soon became universal. So great was the commercial and financial success of these early canals that those fortunate enough to hold shares in them found themselves with rising dividends which within fifty years had reached quite phenomenal heights.

Boat builders and boat repairers established yards on the canalside to construct the specially designed narrowboats. The Boat Museum at Ellesmere Port is fortunate to have acquired the cash book of Charles Leadbeater, boat builder and repairer of Middlewich and this records his accounts between the years 1811 and 1815. He also worked on farm waggons and we can picture that it was from such a trade as this that the canal-boat builders started. Most of the work was in repairs but he did build two boats within this period, one for Mr John Smith of Tunstall, for £154 without stove or sidecloths, and one for Messrs Bradley and Co of Birmingham, complete with stove, cloths and every accessory. The latter included an item, 'Paid for ale by your orders for launching £1'. As ale was twopence a pint (less than 1p), it appears that there were several gallons consumed! The item 'workmanship' was £30 and the rates of the staff of four men and a boy show that they took between five and six six-day weeks to complete the work. A further point of interest is the detail in which the materials were recorded. The lengths of timber for the bottom strake of one of the boats show that it would have been considerably less than seventy feet long, the maximum length able to use Trent & Mersey locks.

It was partly the commercial success of the early canals and partly the need for better communications for the growing requirements of industry that sparked off the next great period of canal building. This is known as the canal mania and it lasted throughout the 1790s. Very many canal Bills were sent to Parliament in the two years 1792 and 1793, though not all were enacted, and not all the authorised canals were built. A great mileage of canals was started though many years were to elapse before the work was completed. Enthusiasm at this time is exemplified by the case of the Rochdale Canal where the necessary, very considerable, sum of money was promised within a few hours of the time advertised that the shares would become available.

Whereas engineering had been the main problem facing the constructors of the early canals it was the labour force during the canal mania. Contractors competed with one another for skilled men and labourers since there were not enough to do the work required. The expanding industries were sucking in workmen and, in addition, the country was soon to be at war with the French. Wages rose and inflation set in. Canal companies had to promote additional Acts of Parliament to raise more money and the greatly increased costs ensured that no canal of this period was able to pay dividends comparable to those built earlier. However, the canal network as we know it was largely completed in the first decade of the nineteenth century.

The third period of canal building in England was in the 1820s and 1830s. This was largely the construction of links such as the Macclesfield Canal and the south Shroppie and the improvement of main lines such as the north Oxford and the Birmingham Canals. It continued into the middle of the nineteenth century in the Black Country with the Tame Valley Canal and others and all these late navigations have one particular feature. Railway competition had already begun and these canals were constructed in as straight a line as possible, ignoring the contours, cutting through hills and striding over low ground on high embankments. Locks were grouped together to waste as little of the boaters' time as possible. Once this period was past there was very little canal construction in the country and, unlike the Continent, very few improvements. The Manchester Ship Canal was built at the end of the nineteenth century, but this was a totally different conception, being an ocean seaway, more like the Suez and Panama Canals.

By the 1820s and 1830s, the canal system had become a complete network and boats were often far from home for weeks and even months at a time. It was then that we find boaters' families beginning to accompany their menfolk. The wife acted as mate and the original mate took charge of a boat of his own. The family boat had arrived.

It is, I think, no coincidence that the painted boat would appear to date from this period. Pictures of earlier narrowboats show that they had little decoration and were painted very simply. Lewery suggests in *Narrow Boat Painting* (see Bibliography) that when the boatman's wife came to live on board she would not have been satisfied with the plain, undecorated cabin that had sufficed the men but instead would want colour and cosiness. We do not know when the first roses and castles appeared, for the earliest description is dated 1858 and neither do we know where they came from. Lewery once more suggests the most likely places. He notes that there were many boat-building and repair yards in both the Potteries and the Black Country. People were employed in pottery painting and in the decoration of painted furniture, faces of clocks and cheap papier-mâché trays and the motifs used were similar to those found in boat decoration. Such people might find temporary work in boatyards, brightening up the insides of cabins. The lacework and curtains would be made by the boatmen's wives and the tiny cabin would soon look much more like home. The diamonds on the outside could have been the company's trade mark and the 'round circles', as a boatman once named them, and anchors would suggest themselves to any painter.

In the past, some authors have suggested that the colourful decoration is of gypsy origin but there is no evidence for this. Hanson in *The Canal Boatmen* (see Bibliography) clearly shows that the boat people themselves were not of gypsy extraction and that the painting on gypsy caravans is quite different. Furthermore, Lewery describes how gypsies were tent dwellers until the middle of the nineteenth century and the painted caravan did not appear until much later than the painted boat.

Painting on the wider barges such as those on the Leeds & Liverpool Canal is quite different again. Barge canals did not form a network throughout the country and those in the north of England had locks of different lengths. Thus the bargemen were seldom far from home or away for long and the family barge was rare.

The interior of the narrowboat living cabin was a wonderful example of economic use of space. Approximately ten feet or less in length and little over six feet at its widest, it included everything necessary for a small family to live in.

Three of the girls trained to crew the boats during World War II give excellent descriptions of living conditions in books that each has written (see the titles by Woolfitt, Smith and Gayford in the Bibliography). The double bed was across the boat at the far end and in daytime the mattress and bedding were rolled up, and the centre of the bed hinged to form the door of a cupboard. There was another cupboard above and a clothes drawer beneath. On the left was the stove used for both cooking and heating; beyond was a crockery cupboard whose door was hinged at the bottom to allow it to fold down and become a table. There was a small drawer beneath for cutlery and a little cupboard at the bottom which could hold pans. The side bed was opposite, with either a drawer or a locker beneath, and a small cross-plank could replace the bed centre to provide seating at the table. Small cupboards and recesses were on both sides of the doorway and a tiny drawer high on the left was used for tickets and similar papers needed at short notice on the trip. The step down also formed the coalbox and a rag rug gave comfort on the floor. A brass paraffin lamp on a hinged arm was used for lighting and brass handles, rails and knobs, all highly polished, were fixed wherever possible. Water was carried in large painted metal cans on the roof and these were filled from taps at the lock cottages and a painted dipper hung on a hook for the boater to take additional water from the canal.

Such a cabin would have been comfortable for a man and his wife and one child; a few boats had a small fore cabin in which two children could sleep. In this century many boats went in pairs, the motor towing the butty. The motor cabin was normally a little smaller than that in the butty but three children could easily sleep in it. In the last century there was often considerable overcrowding with children sleeping in the hold amongst the cargo but similar conditions were also to be found on land. A small family could live comfortably and cosily in a well-maintained boat.

We are often told that canals enjoyed a relatively brief

period of success, lasting perhaps eighty years at the most, and that their days were over when the railway system became established in the 1840s. A study of the records of canals and river navigations in the north-west of England shows that this was not the case in that area. In fact, many canals were busier in the 1880s than they had been fifty years earlier. It further shows that it was the internal-combustion engine that spelt their commercial doom. As far as the railways were concerned, there were several good reasons for the canals' survival and it is worthwhile examining each type of navigation separately.

The navigations fall into three categories: navigable rivers, barge canals and narrow canals. Of the rivers, the courses of the Mersey and Irwell were occupied by the Manchester Ship Canal; the Douglas was bought up and finally superseded by the Leeds & Liverpool Canal and the Weaver was constantly improved (indeed, this is still the case and it can now accept 1,000-ton ships as far as Anderton).

The barge canals were also able to compete successfully with the railways. Before the Liverpool & Manchester Railway was opened in 1831, the Bridgewater Canal carried around 700,000 tons of goods; its best profit was made in 1824 and exceeded £80,000. Profits dropped markedly with the opening of the railway but tonnages of cargo increased, topping the million tons in 1840 and two million tons in 1885! This sort of tonnage was maintained until World War I but it then dropped rapidly to give way to pleasure traffic today. Even the passenger traffic on the Bridgewater Canal and the Mersey & Irwell Navigation was not entirely lost to the much faster railways. In 1891 'Mancunian' wrote in the *Ship Canal News* of conditions in Manchester in 1840:

> The scene of departure and arrival of the Old Quay packets, ere the superior speed and greater convenience of the railway took over from the old river its passenger traffic, was an animated one, our fathers not caring for the breakneck speed offered nowadays!

In fact, swift packets were introduced in 1843 and continued to make profits for a further ten years. In a later article on the Bridgewater Canal in the same publication, Mancunian commented:

> It was a treat to see the swift packet 'The Water Witch' pass on her way to or from Runcorn, doing the journey of 33 miles in three and a half hours, the packet horn giving bargemen warning of its approach.

With regard to freight carriage, the railways had to break into existing traffic flows. The canal companies had years of experience and specialised knowledge with warehouses on site and a network of agencies, all of which had been built up before railways could compete on an equal footing. Furthermore, the industrial towns and cities of the North West and Midlands were growing steadily and trade was expanding so that there was enough work for both forms of transport throughout the century.

The Sankey Navigation (St Helens Canal) and the Manchester, Bolton & Bury Canal were differently placed for both were dead ends and each tapped productive coal mines. Though both were linked with railways, each continued to carry around half a million tons of coal annually throughout the nineteenth century. Again, the traffic diminished in this century and both canals have now been abandoned.

The Leeds & Liverpool and Rochdale Canals were both trans-Pennine navigations though most of their traffic was restricted to one or other side. The Rochdale Canal had remained independent and maintained its volume of cargoes throughout the nineteenth century. The Leeds & Liverpool Canal also kept clear of railway domination and maintained its cargoes though total revenue dropped. Once more, this century has seen the end of practically all commercial carrying and all but a mile of the Rochdale was abandoned in 1952.

Canals: the background

Most of the narrow canals were leased or bought out completely by railway companies which were competing strongly with one another. Thus, when the LNWR leased the Shropshire Union Canal in 1846 it extended itself deeply into Great Western Railway territory. Further, when it was charged heavy dues in Liverpool, it developed and mechanised its canal docks at Ellesmere Port. The railway that was to become the Great Central acquired the Ashton, Peak Forest and Macclesfield Canals which carried it deeply into LNWR country. Yet another instance of this was the important Trent & Mersey Canal, purchased by the North Staffordshire Railway Company, itself a rival of the LNWR. The result of this was that all were well maintained and their volume of cargoes remained high throughout the nineteenth century, to drop away in this century. With the coming of motor transport which could carry from door to door, both railways and canals suffered.

New uses
Because of the rapid post-war decline in commercial carrying, many canals fell into disuse and were in grave danger of abandonment. Already, in 1944, the LMSR Company had obtained an Act of Parliament to abandon such beautiful canals as the Newport and Montgomeryshire branches of the Shroppie, the Huddersfield Narrow Canal and even the Llangollen. Fortunately, it was the latter's water-carrying capacity from the Dee above Llangollen which halted the destruction of the canal and eventually saved it. Several other canals were similarly threatened and the beautiful Kennet & Avon Canal, already unnavigable, nearly went the same way. There were even times when the south Oxford and the Macclesfield Canals were in similar danger and the beautiful but derelict Stratford Canal was only saved from complete destruction by a canoeist. He had kept his ticket which showed that he had actually navigated the canal within a three-year period before Warwickshire County Council

announced that it would seek a warrant of abandonment on the grounds of non-use!

There have been three factors which have saved the canal network as we know it today. L. T. C. Rolt cruised the canals just before the last war and wrote *Narrow Boat* which became an instant success. It caught the imagination of a great many people including Robert Aickman and Charles Hadfield who got together with a few others to found the Inland Waterways Association (IWA) in 1946. In the early years the association campaigned both inside and outside Parliament for the retention of the whole canal system and public meetings and protest cruises were held. Though a few more canals were lost, the majority were saved. The second factor was the steady rise in pleasure cruising. This was unimportant in the 1950s but it gathered momentum in the next two decades. It was fortunate that the IWA was in existence during the gap between the fall in commercial carrying and the rise in the popularity of pleasure cruising; and, furthermore, that such disasters as the collapse of major tunnels did not occur during this period. In the 1960s Barbara Castle was the first government minister to recognise fully the amenity value of canals and although the right to navigate was lost in the 1968 Transport Act it was then agreed to maintain much of the network for pleasure cruising.

Three categories of navigation were to be recognised: the major ones for commercial use, the 'cruiseways' for pleasure boating and the remainder waterways which were to be treated in the most economical way. It was with these last that the third saving factor appeared – the volunteer restoration societies.

Little groups of enthusiasts formed themselves into societies whose object was to improve remainder waterways and to save and to restore many that were already abandoned. The success of these volunteers has already led to the upgrading of several remainder waterways and others are being actively and successfully restored. I was myself involved in the fifteen-year campaign to restore the Lower Peak Forest, Ashton and western section of the Rochdale Canals through Manchester. At the successful conclusion in 1974 the minister, Denis Howell, said that the time had now come not simply to restore such waterways but to build new ones! A happy thought if this is ever carried out.

A further event occurred to bring together and organise the active volunteers and this was the production of a bimonthly publication known originally as *Navvies' Notebook*, and later shortened to *Navvies*. This recorded the names and addresses of organisers and secretaries of volunteer societies and noted the dates, times and places of their operations. It was the brainchild of Graham Palmer and was to lead to the formation of the Waterways Recovery Group (WRG). The group has organised a number of major restoration weekends, attracting as many as 1,000 people from all over the country. It also runs summer camps on specific sites for volunteer enthusiasts. It has been able to purchase equipment and has carried out highly professional work. The group has now linked up with the IWA, which has made major grants for particular restorations. Volunteers find that there is the greatest satisfaction in digging out rubbish from derelict locks and clearing the channel and towpath so that the canal can come once more to life.

As a result of all this work and enthusiasm the canals which fell into disuse with the demise of commercial traffic are now reviving steadily. Canals once derelict are once more linked with the network and each year a few extra miles of lost waterways are regained. Inevitably, the way of life of the narrowboat people has all but vanished, though much of it is still preserved in such places as the Boat Museum, the Black Country Museum and Stoke Bruerne. There are still a few people willing to work the long hours necessary and to live in the restricted conditions for the independence that this life brings. For most of us, the waterways offer peace and a view of the countryside seldom seen from the busy roads.

2

HOW AND WHERE
TO CRUISE

Canal cruising has now become a popular way to spend a
holiday and advertisements for such regularly appear in the
press, whilst painted boats on quiet waters are used to
advertise all manner of commercial products. Nevertheless,
it is still difficult to know where to go for a first cruise and
what sort of boat will best suit the family.

Canals run up hill and down dale, stepping up and down
the slopes by locks which may occur singly or in flights. If
the country is hilly there may be many locks, and before
choosing a canal to explore it is worth considering whether
you want a lot of hard work or would prefer to cruise peacefully with few interruptions. An elderly couple may wish for
few or no locks at all while a family with teenage children
will need locks to keep the crew interested.

'Easy' canals
There are some canals which keep on one level for many
miles and provide an almost lockfree trip. When the Lancaster Canal was built the whole of its southern pound from
Preston to beyond Lancaster was cut into the Lancashire
Plain and this presents a cruise of over forty miles without a
lock. The short branch from Galgate to Glasson Dock has six
locks and at the northern end it is possible to walk up the
abandoned Tewitfield locks to the summit pound. This is not
now navigable except for short lengths and these only for
small boats. The whole 57 miles with only the one flight of
locks was used in the last century by fast packet boats, horse-
drawn passenger boats where the horses galloped at 10mph

and were changed every half-hour at stables on the canalside. For those choosing to cruise today the speed limit is restricted to 4mph and there is no chance of meeting a galloping horse on the towpath or a fast packet in a bridgehole.

Much of the Coventry and north Oxford Canals, together with the whole of the Ashby, lie on one level. There is a stop-lock at Hawkesbury dividing the Coventry from the Oxford but the total length of level water is over fifty miles. The whole of the Bridgewater Canal is completely lockfree, as is the northern length of the Trent & Mersey. The two together provide some fifty-five miles with only the stoplock at the Dutton end of the Preston Brook tunnel. A further gentle cruise is the Macclesfield and upper Peak Forest, 24 miles of level water at over 500ft above sea-level on the side of the Pennines. The Peak Forest Canal was built just before the turn of the eighteenth century and it contours the steeply sloping hills. The Macclesfield Canal was one of the last of the English network and was kept as short and straight as possible. It strides across deep valleys on long embankments at treetop height and slices through bluffs in cuttings. The twelve Bosley locks are amongst the best kept and easiest flights in the country and they present the boater with a further 10 miles of level cruising. The lower pound is still 400ft above sea-level, with long views across the Cheshire Plain.

All these 'easy' canals are well supplied with hire fleets and a peaceful week's cruising can be had with little or no work to do.

'Difficult' canals

At the other extreme, there are canals with many locks and swing bridges which will keep even the most active crew busy. Examples of these include the Leeds & Liverpool (p 74) and the canals which climb up onto the high ground around Birmingham. The Worcester & Birmingham Canal drops down 58 locks in a mere 15 miles to reach the Severn, and the Stratford-upon-Avon Canal leaving the same level has 54 locks in approximately the same distance. The run down the Peak Forest, Ashton and Rochdale Canals through Marple, Romiley and Ashton to Manchester and onto the Bridgewater Canal includes 43 locks in 17 miles. The 35 locks between Middlewich and Kidsgrove on the Trent & Mersey Canal have long been known as Heartbreak Hill!

Cruising a ring
Many people, welcoming the interest of locking, plan their holiday to cruise round a ring. By doing this they travel throughout over fresh ground, which has its attractions even though a return over the same length looks quite different from the opposite angle. For those proposing to cruise a ring of canals, it must be emphasised that a point of no return will be reached when it is less distance to go forward than to go back. If some hold-up occurs or the going is slower than was expected, the holiday may end in a rush. If the cruise is planned to reach some point – for example, Llangollen, Ellesmere Port, Lechlade or perhaps Sharpness – and to return by the same route, it is possible to turn back sooner if progress has been slower than expected.

Examples of such rings are many. The Cheshire Ring takes in the Macclesfield, Peak Forest, Ashton, Rochdale, Bridge-water and Trent & Mersey Canals and the boater can start and finish at any point. In planning to cover this route there are certain factors which must be taken into account. In high summer there is often a water shortage on the highest levels and the Marple and Bosley locks are closed early, perhaps at 4pm, and the boater arriving after this time must then wait until next morning. Water levels on the highest pound may be low and this can add two or three hours to the cruising time of a deeper-draught boat.

The Four Counties Ring includes the Staffs & Worcs, the Trent & Mersey, the Middlewich branch and the Shropshire Union Canals and is an extremely popular route. Its very popularity can cause lengthy hold-ups at some of the locks and add several hours to the cruising time. The route also includes the long Harecastle tunnel whose width is only sufficient for boats in one direction at a time. Here again the boater may have to wait some time and at weekends, when the tunnel-keepers are off duty, boats are permitted to travel north in the morning and south in the afternoon. The boater must wait until the next day if he or she arrives at the wrong time.

The Stratford Ring is another popular cruise and it includes the Avon, the Severn, the Worcester & Birmingham Canal and the Stratford Canal. As has already been noted these two canals are amongst the most heavily locked in the country and there may be lengthy hold-ups. If the boat ahead is in the hands of careful and rather timid people each lock may take twice as long to pass. In this case it is no good feeling frustrated and losing all the joy of cruising through beautiful countryside. We try to help the people ahead, offering to close the gates behind them and even preparing a lock further ahead.

There are several possible rings through Birmingham, all heavily locked but all of interest. The hold-ups described above are of no account if the boater is prepared to start cruising a little earlier. We normally cruise for about seven hours each day and my log shows that each of these rings can be covered comfortably in a week. If we are held up we are prepared to start earlier next morning and still have plenty of time for meals and shopping. For the inexperienced boater, however, we would strongly recommend taking a fortnight instead of a week. This will then give time to stop for perhaps a whole day in some place of especial interest or beauty. It will also allow side excursions, for instance to Whaley Bridge from the Cheshire Ring, or to Ellesmere Port or up the Caldon Canal from the Four Counties Ring. With more time to spare, much longer rings can be planned but the time element and the possible hold-ups must be watched.

29

Planning

Having suggested both easy- and hard-working trips, it is worth discussing how such a holiday may be planned. The speed limit on canals is 4mph but the actual speed depends both on the canal itself and the boat. Our 40ft steel boat with a 13hp diesel engine will go at 4mph on the Grand Union and Bridgewater Canals, 3½mph on the Trent & Mersey and the Shroppie but less than 3mph on the Macclesfield and the Leicester Grand Union summit. In fact, the speed of a boat depends on its shape and on the depth of water on which it is cruising. Any boat will travel much faster on a deep river than on a shallow canal. There is a maximum speed at which a boat will travel and to accelerate the engine further will simply drag back water beneath and around the boat and give no extra pace. Furthermore, this operation will damage the banks, drawing water away from them and causing waves to follow behind. At the first sign of this happening the accelerator should be retarded until the boat moves smoothly through the water. Smaller craft, drawing less water, will travel faster on a shallow canal and the larger boat should always be prepared to slow down, pull over and beckon them by. It is extremely frustrating to follow a very slow boat and if its steerer is competent, he will give way.

The point of this discussion is to show that it is difficult to calculate how many hours it will take to traverse a particular length of canal. Time through locks is also difficult to forecast. With everything in favour it is possible to go through a flight of twelve narrow locks in an hour and we once descended the Bosley flight, consisting of twelve locks, in 55 minutes. When all the locks were in their favour the professional boaters used to call it a 'good road'. However, there may be another boat going down ahead of you, in which case every lock has to be filled before you can use it. With a good locking team this need not make a lot of difference but I have so often seen every member of the crew climb back on board after each lock and take up more time to go ashore again. Wide locks hold twice as much water as narrow locks and usually take more time to empty and fill, and their gates are often much heavier. All these factors should be taken into account when planning the trip. There is an old rule of adding miles of canal to be traversed to the number of locks to be passed and dividing the total by four. This can give a good approximation in hours and we have found it fairly accurate on most canals. It does not work on the heavily locked sections.

Hiring boats
There are many good hire firms throughout the canal system and on the more popular cruising rivers. It is therefore advisable to decide on the type of cruising holiday and the most suitable areas to cruise and then to find a hire firm on that waterway. It is always worthwhile to visit the hire-boat base beforehand and to see the boats, since they may vary in many particulars. If this is not feasible, an experienced cruising friend may be able to give advice. Obviously, a blind booking may well produce an excellent boat, for standards of hire craft throughout the country are fairly high; it is just that boats do vary. The majority of hire firms belong to APCO (the Association of Pleasure Craft Operators) and an unfortunate hire from one of its members should be reported.

Basic boat handling
Most hire firms keep their boats in some form of marina and at the time of starting there will be plenty of bustle for boats will have come in that morning from the previous week's cruising. They will have been cleaned, filled with water and fuel and checked to see that everything is ready for a further week. Some firms have many boats and all may have to be turned round in a few hours. The new hirer drives into the carpark and reports to the office. If the boat is ready, the crew goes aboard and loads up baggage, food and all necessities. It is at this point that it is worth making sure that you know

how to work the boat. Every question should be asked, for once you have started you are on your own. Hire firms try to ensure that the boater is satisfied, but some are so keen to get started that they realise too late that they lack certain essential pieces of information. I am told that a frequent question is, 'Where are the brakes?' Of course, there are none but the engine can be put into reverse to stop the boat, though it cannot be stopped suddenly. I was told of a boater who believed that the boat would go ahead in forward gear, astern in reverse and would stop in neutral! He was somewhat shaken when he put the gear lever into neutral and rammed the lock gates. The secret of avoiding bumps in locks and at canal junctions is to take things slowly for then the boat can be brought more easily under control.

Unfortunately, people throw rubbish into canals, particularly from bridges, and this can be picked up by the propeller and stop the engine. I am reminded of a song by the Gas Street Revivalists which finishes with the words, 'With yards and yards of poly, an antiquated brolly and a supermarket trolley on the blades'. One is very unfortunate to pick up more than one of these objects at a time but we have collected a spring mattress, an inner tube and even some barbed wire on occasions. If there is any likelihood of rubbish beneath a bridge, the gear lever should be put into neutral and the boat allowed to drift through. In this way, the stern will rise slightly and the motionless propeller will not be damaged.

Most boats have a weed hatch which can be lifted so that one can get a hand down to the propeller. The engine must always be switched off first and such items as weed, string and polythene bags can usually be dislodged fairly easily. When the propeller and its shaft have been cleared, the weed hatch must be replaced. People sometimes leave it off and this can be fatal, for the propeller – particularly in reverse – will fling water up into the boat; I know of several cases where a vessel sank for this reason. Another way of clearing the propeller is to bring the boat to a bridgehole or narrows

(*above*) Barrel-vaulted lock-keeper's cottage and split bridge (to allow the towrope to pass) on the heavily locked Stratford Canal, part of the Stratford ring; (*below*) Preston Brook tunnel, Dutton, at the western end of the Trent & Mersey Canal

and feel round it with a boathook from the towpath. If the obstruction is quite immovable, the hire firm should be contacted by phone. They will want to know the whereabouts of the boat and this is where the bridge numbers are useful. In a breakdown of any sort it is worth towing the boat on or back to a bridge which is crossed by a road, not by a farm track. The mechanic can then reach the boat easily with his vehicle.

Using locks

It is now worth commenting on locking. The principle of the lock is simple for it consists of a rectangular chamber built of brick or stone – or occasionally wood or even turf – with a gate or pair of gates at each end. Sluices, closed by doors, let water into the lock from the top and out from the bottom. There are either ground paddles – short tunnels from the canal into the lock – or gate paddles, which are rectangular holes in the gate fitted with a sliding cover. The paddle gear itself varies throughout the country. The commonest are rectangular doors in slots which can be raised or lowered by turning a geared rod with a windlass which the boater carries with him. There are two common sizes of windlass: the smaller, used on most of the narrow canals and on hydraulic paddle gear, and the larger, used on the Grand Union Canal and on certain other waterways. The windlass is a precious item and should always be carried around. It should never be put down or thrown across the lock to someone on the other side, for many are lost each year this way. We carry a magnet on a length of rope and more than once we have retrieved a windlass from the depths for some unfortunate boater.

(*opposite top*) Winter cruising (Boxing Day, 1984) on the Macclesfield Canal past Clarence Mill, Bollington; (*centre*) high summer on the Thames at Windsor, with Swan Upping (marking the Livery Companies' swans) in progress; (*bottom*) Knowle locks on the Grand Union Canal. These wide locks replaced the narrow flight (seen on the left) in the 1930s

When descending a lock, a member of crew should be put ashore in good time to fill the chamber and open the top gate or gates. When the boat is in the gates are closed and the paddles wound right down. I emphasise this for I have often found a top ground paddle left a few notches up; when this happens the lock will either not empty completely or be slow to empty and the bottom gates difficult to open. In any case, water will be wasted and the pound above lowered, particularly if it is a short one. In warm summer weather, when the canals are at their busiest, it is all the more important to ensure that no water is wasted. When the lock is empty the bottom gates will open easily for the boat to cruise out. The gates are then closed again and the paddles wound right down. There is a great temptation to close one or more paddles before the gates are opened but this can slow up the locking, especially when the lock has leaking gates. On certain rivers, such as the Soar, there is no need to close gates on leaving the lock, for loss of water through leaking gates is of no importance.

There is one part of the lock which must be watched carefully when a boat is descending: the sill. The top gates swing onto the sill, which stands a short distance into the lock and is uncovered as the water falls. If the boat is too far back the rudder or propeller may be caught and damaged on the sill. There have even been cases where the whole stern of the boat has lodged on the sill. If this happens the boat will tilt forward rapidly and may even plunge into the depths! Those working the paddles must keep a constant watch for this danger; if it occurs, they should immediately drop the paddles and reflood the lock to float off the boat.

There are other points to watch when rising in a lock. The lock is emptied, the bottom gates opened and closed again when the boat is inside. Bottom paddles are wound right down. A full-length narrowboat (normally 70ft long and 7ft wide) will occupy the whole length of a narrow lock but most modern cruisers are shorter and there are two recommended positions. The boat may either nose the bow fender on the sill of the lock and remain there with the engine ticking over in forward gear, or stay right at the back of the lock with the stern fender against the gates. In the forward position, care must be taken to see that the nose of the boat does not catch under any projection. My daughter once saw a large cruiser lift the gate inches off the sill! However, this is rarely possible except in a wide lock. In the centre of the lock or, in a very few cases, even at the back the flow of water from the sluices can draw the boat towards the top gate. Once a heavy boat starts to run forward, it is almost impossible to hold it and the bump at the top can throw pottery off tables and shelves. Trent & Mersey locks have a bad reputation for this and we take a stern rope onto a bollard if there is one or round the bottom gate beam itself.

When the boat is in the lock and the gates are closed the top paddles are raised. If the boat is properly in position, and any necessary rope is secured, the paddles can be opened fully. Many boaters have been warned to raise the paddles a little only at first but this makes for very slow filling and should be unnecessary. One must always be wary, however, of the enthusiastic boater waiting above who flings up the paddles before you are prepared. I always ask them to leave the paddles to me. Once out of the lock the gates are closed and the paddles wound right down again.

The boater should always be on the lookout for another boat approaching. If on leaving a lock you meet a boat, the gates should be left open for it but the paddles should still be wound down. If you reach a lock which is against you and a boat is approaching from the opposite direction, you should open the gates for it and only take the lock when it has come through. There are few things more annoying than to have a lock filled in front of you when you are approaching from below.

Sometimes it is not possible to open gates fully and occasionally they will not close tightly. This is usually due to

37

rubbish, often timber, getting behind the gate or onto the sill. Timber behind the gate can usually be dislodged by swinging the gate backwards and forwards. Rubbish on the sill can be more difficult and it may be necessary to poke about with a long shaft or a keb, a rake with long prongs, if there is one available.

Dropping down wide locks is very little different from using narrow ones, but rising up in them introduces a further difficulty. A single narrow cruiser in a wide lock is apt to be bumped about, with first the bow swinging across and then the stern. If it is possible for two boats of similar size to use them together, each will keep the other in place. We have also found that using only the paddles on the same side as the boat has solved the problem. If the boat is taken in on the left, we have raised first the ground then the gate paddle on that side and the boat has risen steadily against the wall. After a while, the paddles on the right can be raised.

The help of a lock-wheeler is a great advantage on flights of locks, where the intervening pounds are short. When the commercial boats were running, the lock-wheeler was a member of the crew on a bicycle who rode ahead to prepare each lock. Today it is most often done on foot. This member must always look to see if there is anyone approaching and it may mean peering under a bridge. Cases occur where enthusiastic lock-wheelers, often children, prepare two or even three locks ahead and when you reach the lock, their boat is not even in sight.

Owing to leaky gates, or more often to paddles not being properly wound down, the boater may reach a low pound or even one that is quite empty. When this happens, it is first necessary to find out the cause of the trouble and, if it is a simple thing, like a raised paddle, to put it right. Then water can be brought down from the pound or pounds above, care being taken not to lower their levels too much. The correct way to bring water down is to open paddles at both ends of the lock above. Some people open lock gates at one end and raise the paddles at the other. This is not advisable, for the flow of water may wash pebbles and other rubbish onto the sill thus preventing the gates from closing completely. Low or empty pounds should be reported to the lock-keeper who will check the whole flight.

Tunnels
Tunnels are a further hazard or item of interest depending on the views of the boater. Canals crossing hills or ridges must either be taken over, round or through them. On many canals, both wide and narrow, the tunnels were built sufficiently wide for two narrowboats to pass one another. In such cases, the steerer should ensure that the headlamp works and that it is set at a proper angle before entering the tunnel. The type and angle of the headlamp is important, for some craft are equipped with large, powerful beams that light up the whole tunnel but dazzle any oncoming boat. This is the most common cause of collisions. A wide-beam foglamp, set at a slight angle upwards to illuminate walls and ceiling, is all that is needed. On entering the tunnel the lamp seems to give little light, but once inside the eyes adjust themselves and the whole scene, including the water surface in front of the boat, becomes clear. I had no difficulty on one occasion on coming through Harecastle tunnel with a good torch after the headlamp fused on entry.

Certain tunnels are too narrow to permit boats to pass each other; then it is necessary to ensure that the way is clear before entering. At Harecastle there is a tunnel-keeper at each end in contact with one another by telephone. When the tunnel-keepers are off duty there are clear instructions at each end telling the boater when to enter and when to wait, but there are always some people who ignore instructions and cause a jam in the tunnel. We try to plan our passage during the week when the tunnel-keepers are on duty, though at summer weekends there are so many boats waiting to go through that the instructions are normally obeyed.

With this exception, and that of the tunnel at Dudley, there are no other very long narrow tunnels open to navigation. Lapal, Norwood and Butterley have all subsided and been abandoned, and it is possible to see through the shorter tunnels and make sure that the way is clear. The Boat Museum staff on separate occasions brought a Yorkshire keel and a river tug over the Leeds & Liverpool Canal; on going through its two tunnels they had a crew member at the far end of each to hold up any approaching craft as the two boats could not have passed. Both trips were made in the winter and in each case the engineer in charge was notified.

Rules of the road
The rule of the canal is to keep to the right and to meet another boat port to port. There is a system of signals that all should know (and very few do!) to indicate certain movements to the approaching boat. If we are about to moor on the left bank and want to pass starboard to starboard we should give two toots on our horn and the approaching boat should give two toots in reply. A deep-draught boat may also need to pass on the wrong side and the signal of two toots should be given and answered. It is sometimes necessary to reverse for some distance and three toots should be given, for a narrowboat going backwards is less easy to control. This allows the oncoming boat to prepare to take avoiding action. Four toots are given when the boat itself is out of control. I found this particularly useful when towing a narrowboat from Marple to Ellesmere Port one Easter. On several occasions we met a boat as we approached a bridge-hole. As the boat that I was towing had no engine and could not reverse, it was difficult to stop to let the oncoming boat through and impossible for the latter to get through between my boat and its tow. The signal was appreciated and we were given right of way.

Running aground is a hazard on all canals, particularly when the pounds are low. When this happens it is best to try to get the boat off using reverse; as the boat begins to move backwards, a crew member should be ready at the bows to push off into deeper water. The most difficult position to be aground is amidships, for the stern and bows will pivot sideways, swinging first one way and then the other. It is then best to get a crew member ashore if possible, for it is much easier to push from the towpath than from the side of the boat. On occasions, I have put on thigh boots and stepped into the canal to push off from the shallow water.

It is annoying to see moored boats cast off when a boat is about to overtake them. No doubt they have in mind the flight of locks ahead and the wish to get there first. The boater is probably a motorist and would never dream of pulling out from the kerb in front of a passing car but will do this gleefully in a boat. As the moored boat is approached, crew members leap out and start pulling up mooring spikes and the steerer starts and revs the engine. When this happens to us, I increase speed and draw water from beneath the offending boat which goes firmly aground. I recall one man on the Oxford Canal – which has sloping sides – setting off so quickly that he shot his bows right out onto the bank! It is obviously pleasant to reach a flight of locks before another boat, especially if it is a 'good road', but this attempt to beat another boat by pulling out in front makes for bad feelings. In the days of commercial carrying, it would have ended in a stand-up fight!

Mooring

On canals one may moor anywhere along the towpath, provided that a clear channel is left for passing boats. In the days of the commercial boats there were special moorings with sufficient depth. There was usually a canalside pub and, in earlier days, stables for the horses. The boaters would make for such moorings and enjoy each other's company round a pleasant bar. Stories are told of evenings of music from a squeeze box and of dancing. Boaters' working hours were long and arduous and the evening stop was the highlight of the day. The canalside inns are still there, though most have been modernised and few retain their atmosphere.

We like to moor in the country, far from civilisation, where we can watch the birds coming in to roost and can enjoy the early morning shared only with cattle and sheep in the fields. Canals vary in depth at the sides and on some navigations there are only a few places where this is possible. On such canals it is worth carrying a long gangplank. On rivers and on such waterways as the Trent & Mersey, the Leeds & Liverpool and the Grand Union, there is plenty of water and we can moor against the bank.

When passing moored boats, the moving boat should slow down; this is particularly important when the passing boat is large and of deep draught. We have been passed so gently by pairs of fully laden narrowboats that we scarcely knew that they were there. On the other hand, a heavy steel cruiser has dragged out our moorings and left us floating in the middle of the canal. It is worth 'springing' the mooring ropes when mooring, especially if it is not possible to get close to the bank, to four spikes, one beyond and one short of the bows and one ahead of and the other behind the stern. This procedure is essential when mooring on navigations used by large craft, such as the Gloucester & Sharpness Canal.

On rivers, the banks may be private and moorings are not available. Sometimes there is plenty of room in lock cuts and the boater is always made welcome at the riverside inn.

We believe in having really good ropes. Cotton lines are becoming more difficult to get, so we use nylon climbing rope – lightweight and exceptionally strong. The ropes used should be longer than the boat, though shorter lengths may be used for mooring. We have sometimes found when mooring in a strong crosswind that is blowing us out that the bows or stern may be secured first. It is then possible to carry a rope the length of the boat from the adrift end and onto the bank, thus enabling that end to be pulled in and moored.

Buying a boat

The first piece of advice that I give to a first-time buyer is to find a suitable mooring. Sometimes a secondhand boat can be bought on a mooring and that mooring may be available. The prospective purchaser may even live by the waterway, with a garden reaching the water's edge. If neither of these possibilities occur, it is essential to book a safe and secure mooring within easy reach of the mooring-owner's dwelling, otherwise the boat is liable to be vandalised. Some farmers allow boats to be moored against a field but they are rarely able to supervise the site. The British Waterways Board is seldom satisfied with such a mooring and it is so much better to be in a properly supervised marina.

It is always difficult to decide on a first boat and it is worth having one or two hire-boat holidays first. Not only can one sample the pleasures and snags of a waterway holiday but one or more types of boat can be tried out too. We had three hire-boat holidays before we bought our first boat, and this was built for us to our own layout. It was constructed of marine plywood but we soon found that it was really too fragile for canal cruising, where bumps are likely to occur – both against other boats and against lock sides. When we had our second (and present) boat built, we knew exactly what we wanted. Constructed of steel, we had the engine installed and the cabin top and sides built for us, but did all the fitting out ourselves. An advantage of this, besides saving money, is the fact that layout changes are very simple, since the position of every screw is known, or whether or not a certain section is glued.

Over the last two centuries, the narrowboat has evolved as a highly suitable canal craft. The earliest vessels were horse-drawn but later steam, and then diesel, engines were installed to provide the power in boats designed to carry around twenty-five tons of cargo. In the heyday of commercial carrying the navigations were dredged to their proper depth to enable the boats to get through. Today, the motor narrowboat, converted for cruising, has most of its weight in the stern. It was designed thus, so that its propeller would still be covered when it was travelling empty. Most converted boats are therefore fairly deep draught and unfortunately many of the more beautiful rural canals are not dredged sufficiently for them to cruise comfortably. Furthermore, the large propeller is close to the bed of the canal and is liable to pick up any rubbish that has been thrown in.

Nevertheless, the narrowboat has its undoubted advantages. It provides more room than any other craft on the narrow canals and it is ideal for the long holiday. When commercial carrying diminished after the war, it was possible to buy well-maintained narrowboats at very low prices. Most of the best craft have now been snapped up for conversion and it is seldom possible to find a bargain. Two contrasting stories may serve to emphasise this. A married couple, both Boat Museum members, found a suitable composite boat – steel sides and elm bottom – and bought it. They spent a fortnight's 'holiday' with the boat out of the water, replacing the bottom timbers and making certain other repairs and then had a first-class boat. Replacing elm planks along the whole length of a 70ft boat, and then caulking and tarring the whole, is no mean feat but the couple knew what they were doing and how to do it.

The other story concerns some wooden boats sold off for a song by the National Coal Board. Many were bought for conversion and each was fitted with an engine and gearbox, and a cabin top built over the hold. One such boat was bought and used for a pleasant summer holiday and then brought up to a mooring on the Peak Forest Canal. After a time, it sank on the mooring. The Fire Brigade helped to pump it out but it soon sank again. Eventually, the Boat Museum was offered it with the proviso that it should be raised and removed immediately. As it was an important hull, this offer was accepted. Volunteers pumped it out, patched the worst cracks, and towed it to Ellesmere Port where it was lifted out onto the bank. The many rotten planks were all replaced, the cabin and power unit removed and the hull restored to its original condition. We were told by boatmen from the canal on which it had worked that these boats were often known to sink if they were left unused for long. When empty, it was not difficult to raise them and no harm was done. Sinking, however, is a different matter when boats have been converted for pleasure cruising, complete as they are with beds and bedding, cupboards full of crockery and a whole lot of personal effects. We have seen several more converted wooden narrowboats, all too often sunk on their moorings.

Many secondhand narrowboats have seen years of service; even the iron and steel ones may have very weak bottoms since they have been dragged, loaded, over stony canal beds. The warning is therefore reiterated: anyone considering buying an ex-working boat should be knowledgeable, experienced and something of a craftsman.

The final comment concerning the purchase of any secondhand boat is that it should be fully surveyed before the transaction is completed. A friend of ours considered buying a nice-looking secondhand boat and we went to see it. It was in the water but it was the driest boat that I have ever seen, with spiders' webs in the bilge. Our friend decided to have a survey and dry rot was found in the bottom! A boat is like a house or a car: any defects should be discovered before purchase.

3

WHEN TO CRUISE

Planning a week's cruising holiday, perhaps for the first time, people may wonder what the different seasons hold in store. Is it better to cruise at Easter; during the spring bank holiday; at the height of the season; in the autumn, or even at Christmas? These times correspond with school holidays but there are also the intervening periods. The actual cost of hire goes up in the busier seasons, but apart from this there are many other factors worth considering. We have cruised each of these times in our own boat and they all have their own advantages and disadvantages.

Easter
Easter may vary from late March to well beyond the middle of April but there is very little difference in the weather. My log shows some March days to have been fine and bright while those in late April and even early May have had snow and hail. In 1981, for example, I recorded both 20 and 21 April as a 'brilliant day, warm and sunny'; while on the 23rd, after a lovely sunset on the previous day, I 'looked out over fields covered with two inches of snow'. The lesson to be learnt is simple: if you plan to cruise at Easter, take warm clothes, wind- and waterproof outer garments, plenty of warm bedding and make sure that the heating arrangements on the boat are adequate and working. We have a small solid-fuel stove which burns practically any type of fuel, including scrap timber, and we carry a small saw and collect dead branches to keep the fire going.

Having coped with weather problems, there are many

advantages to an early cruise. There is usually plenty of water in the canal with levels up and the bywashes flowing around the locks. This may not seem important in a small, light-draught boat, but with a large cruiser or narrowboat a few inches more water in a shallow canal like the Llangollen or the Macclesfield may make a great difference to the cruise. Furthermore, it is much easier to moor at the canalside when the water level is high. The hire boats have just completed their winter maintenance and should be at their best.

Coarse fishing has a closed season between 15 March and 15 June and no anglers are seen on the canals on an Easter cruise. If you had hoped to take out a licence and fish from the boat, Easter is not the time to go. As anglers and boatmen may have conflicting interests, it is nice to cruise along knowing that you will not upset contestants in an angling match.

More important is the fact that there are fewer weeds at Easter than at the season's height. On well-used canals, weed presents little problem but my log records masses of duckweed on the Erewash Canal and on the Springs Branch late in the season. Weed cutting is still carried out on the Fen rivers and large floating rafts of it may present a problem. Air-cooled engines, and those in which the cooling water is circulated inboard, are at an advantage on weedy stretches but it may still form a ball around and behind the propeller.

Each season has its own crop of wild flowers and Easter is no exception. Yellow coltsfoot brightens the towpath, blackthorn appears in the hedges, and the woodlands are often carpeted with wood anemones and celandine and small clumps of primroses bloom in the cuttings. The birds are very busy at this time of year and are more easily seen in the leafless hedges. The beautiful blue flash of the kingfisher is often seen and it is a little less shy than during the busier summer months. Herons appear on most canals, standing still on the bank or in shallow water and making sudden darts with their long beaks to catch a fish. They take flight as the boat approaches, bending the long neck back into an S-shape so that the head rests between the shoulders.

In the water itself, moorhens, coots and wild duck are busy nest-building and the huge rush nests of swans appear in secure places. The larks are singing in the sky and it is a lovely time to be on the water provided that you are well pre-pared for the sudden return of winter.

Early summer
May and early June make for delightful cruising. The weather should be warmer though cold nights can occur and the days are long and light. One of the most pleasant things about boating is that you are out of doors and close to nature throughout the whole day. The early-morning walk along the towpath with the dog, the marvellous atmosphere at the end of the day and the sunset just before bedtime are moments never to be forgotten.

The season is still early, and though there are probably more boats cruising there is still plenty of water and very little weed. The coarse-fishing season has not yet started and the whole waterway belongs to the boater and towpath walker. The trees are all in fresh-green leaf and everything looks so clean. And, if the season is not particularly back-ward, the hedges are ablaze with May blossom giving off its gorgeous scent. The early wild rose may also be in bloom. Cruising then on a sunny day often has a very special magic.

River banks are especially bright with flowers, including many of the commoner species such as ox-eye daisy, poppy, charlock, wild parsley and dandelion. Cowslips bloom in the limestone woodlands and many coloured comfrey can also be seen.

The birds have all hatched their first brood of chicks and pairs of swans swim proudly with a family of cygnets. Mother duck has anything up to a dozen minute ducklings and the tiny fluffy black chicks of the coot rush for safety as the boat comes by. Swallows and martins sweep up and down the waterway catching flies on the wing, and larks still sing as they rise higher and higher into the air.

High summer

High summer is the time when many of us take our holidays. From mid-July until the end of August we can expect, or at least hope for, warmth and sunshine and it is then that families with school-age children plan to spend some time away from home. As in other holiday places, the canals are at their busiest at this time. Some canals, however, are busier than others and certain days of the week are busier at particular spots. Many hirers have to start and finish on a Saturday, though some are able to change over on a different day. This can cause traffic jams at the first lock reached, the congestion only easing when the boats become more spaced out. We have moored below the Hurleston locks on a Saturday evening and watched boats making for the Llangollen Canal. As many are beginners, chaos ensues and we do our best to help sort it out. Similar hold-ups occur at both Foxton and Watford and at some of the narrow tunnels. It is worth remembering that pace on the canals is slow, that the canal holiday is relaxing and that there should be no hurry. Unlike the roads, most bottlenecks are in attractive places and there is a chance to chat with other boaters over a cup of tea.

There may be a shortage of water during a dry summer and with so many boats using the locks the levels may be reduced still further. The larger and deeper-draught boats may even get stuck and they will, in any case, travel more slowly. In mid-afternoon flights of locks may be closed to traffic to save water. Short pounds between locks may be very low indeed owing to leaky locks or paddles not being wound fully down. In the oldest canals, such as the Staffs & Worcs, the variation in lock depth may mean that the pound above a deep lock and below a shallower lock is a foot or more down.

High summer is also very much the anglers' season and

matches are held, particularly at weekends. On these occasions, dozens or even hundreds of anglers are strung out along the towpath at regular intervals and the boatman must be prepared to reduce speed to a minimum until they have been passed. All these considerations – water shortages, hold-ups and slowing down for anglers – must be taken into account when planning a cruise. The boat will either travel less distance or take longer on an August day compared to a day in May.

This is a splendid time for flowers on the towpath and along the canal banks. The scented meadow-sweet grows in profusion and willowherb and true valerian abound, together with masses of the showy Himalayan balsam. Countless other wild flowers deck the hedgerows and a great show of them can be made in a suitable vase, such as the dipper. The rarer plants must not be picked and amongst these are several kinds of wild orchids.

By now the families of water birds are growing up. Cygnets and ducklings are almost as big as their parents, though second-brood ducklings will be darting about. Swallows and martins swoop close to the water and beautiful dragonflies abound. Butterflies are common and the air has a richness of plenty. Altogether, it is a lovely time for the boater who has no particular object in view and is content to allow plenty of time.

Autumn

The autumn is a quieter period and hiring costs are rather less. There is often good weather and the golden days of October can be delightful. Stoppages for canal repairs can start in the autumn but many less-vital ones are held back until the end of October to allow as much time as possible for cruising. The clocks are not put back until late October so the days, though now much shorter, allow a full day's cruising. Anglers are making the best of the weather before winter starts and weeds on the less-used canals may prove difficult.

(*above*) Audlem locks on the Shropshire Union Canal: boats pass one another in the short intervening pounds; (*below*) Anderton Boat Lift today. The metal aqueduct on the right links with the Trent & Mersey Canal. The caissons, counterbalanced by weights, lower the boats to the Weaver

(*above*) Foxton Boat Lift and locks, *c*1907: the lift used an inclined plane; one caisson is at the top near the engine house and chimney. The locks are on the right (*Ware Collection, National Waterways Museum*); (*below*) Brindley's Barton stone aqueduct and Barton lock on the Mersey & Irwell Navigation. Painted by Albert Harris in 1894 from an earlier print, *c*1870 (*City of Manchester Art Galleries*)

4

ENGINEERING FEATURES

Locks

Locks are the most common engineering structures on the waterways, occurring singly, in flights or even in staircases. The principal and operation of modern pound locks has been explained in Chapter 2 so here I shall examine their other interesting aspects.

All the later canal engineers tried where possible to group their locks into flights, for it is quicker for the boater to work from lock to lock than to come upon them singly and separated. Locks in flights were built to a standard depth, so that the water taken from the pound above to fill the lock was replaced when the lock above was emptied. If all locks in a flight are empty it is theoretically possible to come down the entire flight using only one lockful of water. For this to be achieved, the lock below must be filling as the one above is emptying, ensuring that no water is then lost over the bywash. This is important, as every drop of water used in locking must be replaced in the pounds above, and eventually in the top pound.

When canals had to change levels in a short distance on steep-sided hills, staircases of locks were often built, in which the top gates of one lock formed the bottom gates of the one above. There are examples of five-lock staircases in England at Bingley (p79), and two at Foxton (p100); there is also one of eight on the Caledonian Canal in Scotland. Without side ponds, they are very wasteful of water, for any boat approaching from the top when another has just come up must empty the lower locks before dropping down. They can also cause considerable hold-ups since boats cannot pass in a narrow staircase and barges cannot pass in a wide one. The famous three locks at Bratch on the Staffs & Worcs Canal are separated by pounds only a few feet in length and each pound is connected by a channel to a side pond. They remain a bottleneck and, though this does not matter to the pleasure boater, to the commercial boater time was money.

There are now no flash locks or staunches in England. These were the most primitive form of lock, consisting of weirs built across the river, each with a movable gate. The lock consisted of a horizontal beam on the river bed and another movable beam above water level. Vertical planks, or rymers, fitted against the two and a number of these could be withdrawn to give a clear passage. Boats coming down would then shoot through the gap, whilst those waiting to go up would stay until the levels had evened out a little and would then be winched or dragged through. Very wasteful of water, they were never used on canals. However, there were many such flash locks on the Thames; the last at Hart's and at Medley were only removed in the 1930s. Those on the Avon at Fladbury and Pershore lasted until the early 1950s.

Rather more sophisticated staunches were built in the last century on the Fen rivers. They consisted of a small island with a weir on one side and a guillotine gate on the other; the latter could be raised to allow the boats to pass through. A good example can be seen on the Lark at King's Staunch near Mildenhall and, although the gate and weir are both missing, it is easy to picture them in position.

Inclined planes and vertical boat lifts
There are other less wasteful means of accomplishing a change of level on a canal. These include the inclined plane, the vertical boat lift and, in France, the water slope.

Inclined planes
The inclined plane is perhaps the most simple and obvious

method of taking boats from one level to another and was used in China as early as the ninth century. The boats were dragged on rollers up a smooth and even slope and over a mound at the top onto the higher canal level. Planes were very common in England in the late eighteenth and early nineteenth centuries; small boats on the Bude Canal even had wheels. On the Shropshire tub-boat canals, the boats went up and down on cradles which ran on rails, the loaded boats from the top drawing up the unladen ones. There is a fine example at Hay near Coalport on the Severn. It has recently been cleared and restored with the rails relaid as part of the Ironbridge Gorge Museum. A steam engine at the top pulled the loaded boats from the upper canal onto the plane.

The other inclined plane that is well worth a visit is at Foxton near Market Harborough. It was built early in this century to avoid the use of the ten Foxton locks, thus saving both time and water. The plane slopes down sideways from the upper to the lower level and was built on a different principle to the Shropshire planes. Two tanks, known as caissons, full of water and each large enough to hold two narrowboats side by side, were closed at both ends by guillotine gates. They ran sideways on rails, the one descending linked by cables to the one ascending. They were of approximately equal weight except when the lower was running into water at the bottom; this was compensated for by the plane levelling out at the top. In order not to tip the upper caisson at the top, its lower set of wheels ran into trenches. A boat made no difference to the caisson's weight for it displaced its own weight of water. A steam engine was used to set the caissons in motion and their gates were raised hydraulically. The plane was abandoned after a few years when traffic was found to be insufficient to keep the engine in steam. It has recently been cleared by enthusiastic volunteers and the boiler house is presently being restored. The local authority has made a carpark and trail a few hundred yards from the top.

Engineering features

Vertical boat lifts

Several such lifts were tried out on different canals at the end of the eighteenth century. The deep top lock at Tardebigge replaced an unsatisfactory one on the Worcester & Birmingham Canal and another was tried out on the Somersetshire Coal Canal but this too was not considered to be completely satisfactory. Seven small lifts were built on the Grand Western Canal in 1838, each of two caissons counterbalancing one another and each able to take an 8-ton tub-boat. They worked successfully for nearly thirty years. In 1875 the world's first major boat lift was built at Anderton, near Northwich in Cheshire, to link the Trent & Mersey Canal with the River Weaver. It has since had major repairs and certain structural alterations.

The Anderton Boat Lift, as originally designed and built by Edwin Clark for Edward Leader Williams, was planned to work hydraulically. Two tanks or caissons, not unlike those used at Foxton, were placed upon hydraulic rams which passed through bearings into cylinders beneath the ground. The cylinders were interconnected and when one ram descended it forced the other up. The caissons were closed at both ends by guillotine gates. A trough linked the lift with the Trent & Mersey Canal and this was so constructed that the level of water in it was slightly greater than the level outside the bottom caisson. When the top caisson gate was raised, a few inches of water flowed in and when the bottom caisson gate was lifted, a few inches flowed out. In this way, the top caisson was always slightly the heavier and, in theory, all that was needed to make them change places was to release the brakes on the drum. In fact, a small steam pump provided an accumulator with sufficient hydraulic power to start the movement and also to open and close the gates.

The River Weaver is fairly salty and salt water so eroded the bearings that between 1906 and 1908 the entire lift was reconstructed and each caisson was counterbalanced with weights. This entailed the strengthening of the whole structure with a sloping supporting frame and a whole series of pulleys on top. The lift was also electrified and electric winches put in to raise and lower the gates.

The lift is easily reached by road to the village of Anderton and then on foot along the towpath. The land at the bottom is private as it forms part of the British Waterways port of Anderton. Across the river are the huge ICI chemical works of Winnington and Wallerscote. The lift is best appreciated from a boat or from the hillside when boats are ascending or descending.

Tunnels

It was not always necessary to carry a canal over a hill or across a ridge and it was (and still is) often difficult to feed a short, high top pound with water. Frequently, it was more convenient to tunnel through the hill and to run the canal underground. Deep cuttings may have been used but their sloping sides consumed so much surface ground that a tunnel was probably more satisfactory, especially to the land owner.

Two methods of tunnel building were commonly used, the first being the simple 'cut and cover'. A deep cutting was made and the actual tunnel constructed along the bottom. The ground was then put back on top and covered with the soil which had been kept in a separate pile. This method was used for tunnels not far beneath the surface since there is a practical limit to the depth of a cutting.

The second, and more usual method, was to survey the line accurately over the hilltop and then dig a series of shafts of sufficient depth to reach the level of the canal. Two plumb-lines were then suspended down either side of the shaft in the direct line of the canal and this indicated the direction of the headings to be driven on each side of the shaft. Assuming the accuracy of the line, the headings would meet to give a straight tunnel linking the two sections of the canal on either side of the hill. The line was not always quite accurate and some tunnels are crooked. Saltersford, near Northwich, is the shortest tunnel on the northern length of the Trent & Mersey Canal and it is also the most crooked. I know of no tunnel where the headings actually missed one another but the Braunston tunnel has a dog-leg where two headings were off line.

When the long and very deep Standedge tunnel on the Huddersfield Narrow Canal was being built through the Pennines, the deep shafts ran below the water table and the tunnel was largely built from both ends. When sighting with surveying instruments, the line is straight but Standedge tunnel is so long that the water, following the curve of the earth, would have been nearly two feet higher in the centre than at either end. This would have had the effect of the roof being two feet too low in the centre. In order to maintain the right depth of water and height of roof, the water was let in from time to time and the height noted.

For those who cruise the canals, the tunnels occur as an expected feature but for those who journey by car or on foot, it may be difficult to locate even the most easily accessible. Perhaps one of the easiest to find and explore is at Chirk on the Llangollen Canal. Follow a minor road (the B4500) off to the west side of the A5; a small track leads from it down onto the towpath alongside the basin between the tunnel and the aqueduct. The tunnel is just over a quarter of a mile long and the towpath runs through it. It is best to explore with a good torch, though its handrail makes it quite safe.

Most of the longest tunnels are without towpaths and boaters legged their boats through in the early days, the horses being led over the horse path on top. The more attractive end of Standedge is on the Yorkshire side at Marsden. Here it is necessary to leave the A62 and take a turning to the north to the station. Crossing the railway and the infilled top lock, the road runs back westward. The Marsden depot is down on the left in a large gritstone ware-house and the tunnel entrance and restored tunnel cottages are close by. The first impression of so great a tunnel is the smallness of its entrance, made to look even smaller by the presence of two railway tunnels at a slightly higher level, and the great height of the hills that rise above. One of the railway tunnels takes the trans-Pennine line from Manchester to Leeds but the other is disused. The rail tunnels are connected to the canal tunnel at intervals, and in the days of steam smoke puffed out onto the unfortunate boatmen legging below!

Another tunnel worthy of a visit is the Coates end of Sapperton (on the Thames & Severn), recently restored to its former glory. Here, a minor road from Coates (near Cirencester) to Tarlton crosses the canal and a drive runs up to the Tunnel House Inn. The inn has an attractive sign by the roadside showing a boat entering the tunnel. The portal is very impressive, with two hollowed niches which are said to have been intended for Father Thames and Sabrina though they were never filled. The canal was built for Thames barges but the tunnel entrance in the wooded hills looks quite small. The inn was built to provide accommodation for the navvies who worked on the tunnel and it originally had a third storey, long since removed.

Dudley tunnel can be explored by boat from the Black Country Museum. After passing through the two brick-lined sections, the massive limestones can be seen as can the entrance to the old limestone tunnel built to enable stone from under Wren's Nest to be brought out by boat. Netherton tunnel runs parallel to Dudley and is much wider. Built in 1858, it has towpaths on both sides so that two horse-drawn boats could pass.

Some boat passengers become claustrophobic in tunnels and it is usually possible for them to leave the boat and follow the horse path over the top. Tunnels with towpaths have no horse path but it is normally feasible to reach the other end by following byroads. Routes can be planned to avoid tunnels, or, equally, to include several of the longer ones. We once

received a cup for the longest journey distance to a rally
which included twelve miles beneath the ground!

Embankments and aqueducts

Canals cross valleys as well as climbing hills. On early canals
there are several examples of the navigation entering the river
to leave it on the other side. The Oxford Canal does this at
Aynho and Shipton and the Trent & Mersey does the same
below Alrewas. The Caldon makes use of a length of the
River Churnet and the Grand Union allows the Colne to
flow in and out at several points. This is a relatively cheap
method of crossing a river, though a weir is usually necessary
to maintain a sufficient depth of water. There are disadvantages, however: when the river section is in flood it may be
quite impassable and the river itself is likely to deposit
detritus.

Valleys are more usually crossed by embankments and
aqueducts. If the stream is small, it may be carried beneath an
embankment in a culvert but rivers, roads and railways are
usually crossed on aqueducts. A large embankment will have
involved the movement of huge quantities of clay, gravel,
sand and rock and it was usual, where possible, to site the
bank within reach of a cutting to provide the material. The
great cuttings and embankments on the Shroppie are a case in
point, the material being removed from the one to build the
other.

The earliest canal embankments in England were built by
James Brindley on the Bridgewater Canal. Arthur Young
described how Brindley pushed out his bank by building two
parallel wooden channels supported by stilts, along which
could float two boats with a soil-filled hopper resting
between them. The material was dumped and the boats
returned for more.

Embankments of any height are tremendously heavy and
need to settle before the canal is laid along them. In many
cases slips have occurred and the great Shelmore Bank on the

from a minor road south from the A539 east of Llangollen. The same canal has one other great aqueduct, which crosses the Ceiriog valley south of the Chirk tunnel. Once more an iron trough was used but it was encased in masonry. It is a fine and beautiful structure but it is somewhat dwarfed by the higher and later railway viaduct.

Telford also used iron for smaller aqueducts over roads; a good example is to be seen at Stretton (another Stretton!) near Brewood, north of Wolverhampton, where the Shroppie crosses the Holyhead road. There is a similar one on the Macclesfield Canal east of Congleton. He also used this material for bridges and fine examples include Galton bridge over the BCN New Main Line and the two Severn bridges at Holt Fleet and Tewkesbury.

There are many other fine engineering structures on the canal system, several of which are well illustrated in Ransom's *The Archaeology of Canals* (see Bibliography). Most of these can be reached from the towpath except those in private grounds.

5

THE MAIN LINES

Some canals were planned purely for local purposes, perhaps to bring coal from the pits to growing industrial centres or to tap limestone outcrops. Others were intended as main lines from sea to sea or from one big centre of population to another. In the latter case the navigation might have been built in its entirety by one company, or several companies may have built sections which were eventually combined. Three main lines are described here: the Trent & Mersey, 93 miles long; the Leeds & Liverpool, 127 miles; and the Grand Union Canals, 138 miles from Braunston to Brentford and just under 160 miles to Regent's Dock.

The Trent & Mersey Canal

History
When James Brindley's survey of a route between Runcorn on the Mersey and Shardlow on the Trent was accepted as the basis of the Trent & Mersey Canal, he himself named it the Grand Trunk. He considered that it would be a vital artery and that branches would run from it throughout the country. It was the first of the main lines to be built and the planners were faced with a number of major problems which had not previously been met in England. The canal was to link two rivers, one flowing west and the other east. It had therefore to cross the main watershed and climb to over 400ft above sea-level to do so, passing through a major tunnel at Harecastle on the summit level. This was not the first canal tunnel in Europe, for Malpas on the Canal du Midi is nearly 100 years older, but nothing of comparable length had ever

been attempted. The coal measures that make up the strata of Harecastle Hill include tough sandstones, friable shale and seams of coal and little was known of the geology at that time.

At the two ends of the canal, the river navigations were used by the Mersey sailing flats and the Humber keels. A waterway to accommodate both types of craft would have been an advantage, but this was not then considered feasible. There was an existing plan for an alternative route, suitable for such craft, using the Weaver and running through lower country to reach the valley of the River Sow, a tributary of the Trent. This would have avoided tunnelling and would have been cheaper to build. Unfortunately, the line and its link with the Severn avoided the industrial areas that needed it most. Josiah Wedgwood, the pottery manufacturer, was a keen supporter of the Trent & Mersey Canal and it is said that he subscribed a thousand guineas for Brindley's survey. The line through Stoke-on-Trent was the most commercially viable and was therefore the one chosen.

James Brindley had been closely associated with the Bridgewater Canal and its underground links from Worsley Delph to the Duke of Bridgewater's coal mines. The first underground canal was driven northwards into the quarry face and by 1765 it already extended for over a mile. Used partly for drainage, it was built as a navigation for special boats which could operate from the coal seams themselves and from side canals which ran along the strike of the seams. Brindley was familiar with the measurements of this canal: 9ft wide, 8ft high and 3ft 7in deep. He also knew the simple wooden boats, the largest of which were 50ft long and 7ft beam. It is therefore no coincidence that he planned his Harecastle tunnel to be 9ft wide. It is said that the Trent & Mersey boats were first planned to be 6ft 5in beam but this was increased to 7ft before construction commenced. The locks were built a few inches wider than the boats, and long enough to hold a 70ft boat, though not all the early narrowboats were built as long as this. The advantage of these narrow locks over ones twice the width is the fact that they take less water to fill the chamber. This is important on any canal, and particularly one climbing to a high summit.

The Trent & Mersey and the Staffs & Worcs Canals were both surveyed by Brindley and each was authorised by Act of Parliament on the same day in 1766. They were thus the first narrow canals in the country, and set the standard for many of the later canals.

Though the bridges and Harecastle tunnel on the main length of the canal are narrow, the two extremities were built to a wider gauge. The western end, from the junction with the Bridgewater at Preston Brook to Middlewich, has three tunnels at Preston Brook, Saltersford and Barnton. This section was built wide enough for the smaller Mersey flats of 12ft beam. However, it was not wide enough for the duke's barges and two narrowboats cannot pass in the tunnels. The aqueduct over the Dane at Croxton was full barge width, but it has since been narrowed and there is a single wide lock at Middlewich, known as the Big Lock.

The canal was built to full barge width at the eastern end, complete with six wide locks so that barges and the smaller Yorkshire keels could reach Horninglow at Burton-on-Trent. It was then able to compete successfully with the older Trent Navigation to Burton.

The route

Cruising the Trent & Mersey from west to east, we enter from the Bridgewater at Preston Brook. The 1,200yd tunnel was later lengthened by a few yards and the theoretical

(*opposite top*) Stretton aqueduct carrying the Shropshire Union Canal over the A5 Holyhead road. Designed by Telford in 1832; (*centre*) the Chirk aqueduct crosses the Ceiriog valley; (*bottom*) the mighty Pontcysyllte aqueduct carrying the Llangollen Canal over the Dee valley. Chirk and Pontcysyllte were both designed by Telford and use an iron trough, though that at Chirk is encased in masonry

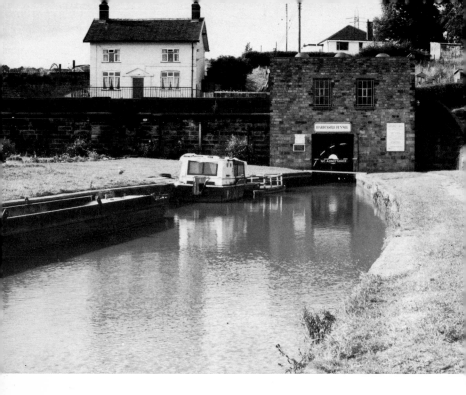

(above) The south end of the narrow Harecastle tunnel. The ventilating fans are above the entrance and the tunnel-keeper's house is on the left; (below) the northern end of the wide Blisworth tunnel with a boat ready to be legged through, *c*1912 *(Ware Collection, National Waterways Museum)*

junction is therefore within the tunnel. The original intention had been to extend the canal right down to the Mersey estuary, but when the Bill went to Parliament the Duke of Bridgewater inserted a clause to allow it to link up with the Bridgewater; this saved the Trent & Mersey Company the cost of the extension and the necessary extra locks. The Bridgewater itself gained, for all boats making for the Mersey had to pay a toll for the few miles they travelled on that canal.

It is possible to see through the tunnel and to make certain that no boat is coming the other way. A horse path runs over the top and boats were originally legged through. Later on, a steam tug – with wheels placed horizontally on both sides to keep it central in the tunnel – towed strings of boats that waited at each end. More recently there were traffic lights but these have not been in use for the last 20 years.

For the next few miles, the canal is cut high on the side of the Weaver valley and there are several splendid views of that navigation lying below. Saltersford and Barnton tunnels are short and crooked but it is possible to see through each to ensure a clear passage. At Anderton the canal and river approach very close to each other, though for a century there was no connection. In 1875, the Anderton Boat Lift (p58) was built so that boats and barges could move freely from one navigation to the other. Beyond Anderton a new, straight length of canal replaces a mile of the old line which subsided into the salt workings below. The Lion Saltworks, which stands on the canalside, uses the ancient method of brine evaporation, and is open to the public throughout the summer months.

The canal begins to climb out of the Weaver valley at Middlewich and 35 locks occur in the next 12 miles, some singly and some grouped together into flights. The branch to the Shroppie (pp128–34) runs off to the south-west below King's lock and the Macclesfield Canal also branches off at the summit. Brindley's original flight to the summit was of single locks but the canal had become so busy by the early nineteenth century that Telford advised that additional locks should be built alongside. Towards the top of the flight, the water begins to change colour to an ochreous brown. The reason for this becomes obvious as the tunnels are approached, for there is a great deal of ochre in the coal measures which is leached out and carried into the channel. In the same way, the Bridgewater Canal is stained with ochre at Worsley.

Brindley's original Harecastle tunnel was to become a serious bottleneck. The boat horses were led over the hill while the boats were legged through the tunnel, which was too narrow for two boats to pass. First Rennie, and then Telford, were called upon to solve the problem. In the 1820s, Telford proposed a second tunnel parallel to the first, this time with a towpath. This was built between the years 1825 and 1827 and is the one in use today.

The run through to Etruria top lock used to be full of interest for narrowboats carrying china clay and flints offloaded at canalside potteries. The names Longport, Middleport and Westport bear witness to the waterborne trade. The navigation passes through the great Shelton Iron & Steel works, now practically closed. When in full operation, crucible trucks would appear full of molten slag, to be tipped like flaming lava into pits. At one point, the canal runs through the corner of a building, and red-hot steel could be seen being rolled into joists and girders. The steel-works grew steadily through much of the last century and the first half of this, some of it on land which had originally belonged to Josiah Wedgwood. His handsome eighteenth-century mansion stands above the canal and was at one time occupied by the iron-and-steel company. The gardens used to sweep down to the canal which was here widened into an ornamental feature. His great Etruria pottery stood beside the canal but all this has now been demolished except for a small round building with circular windows.

72

The Caldon Canal comes in from the north-east above Etruria top lock and the navigation then drops down into Stoke, crossing the River Trent on a small aqueduct. Below Stoke, the canal follows the Trent valley down through delightful rural scenery and passes Wedgwood's huge new factory at Barlaston. The old pottery, brewing and canal town of Stone stands beside its locks with its drydocks and repair yards which are nearly as old as the canal itself. Beyond this, the valley widens, the locks become more spaced out and the river increases in size. Small villages with attractive churches and mansions with extensive parks border the waterway, which at times is itself more like a river. The junction with the Staffs & Worcs Canal is reached at Great Haywood, and the many-arched packhorse bridge leads off to Shugborough Hall.

A 10-mile pound carries the canal through Rugeley, past a coal mine and a power station, and into the deepest of woodlands almost within sight of Lichfield. The Trent itself is crossed on an aqueduct. Fradley junction and the Coventry Canal lie below three locks, and six more locks drop the waterway through Alrewas and into the Trent itself. The river has split into a number of streams, all of which are held up with weirs. The main stream and weir can be quite dangerous when the river is in flood but it is well protected by a barrier.

Leaving the river, the canal skirts the north side of Burton-on-Trent to reach Horninglow wharf, once the very important terminus of the wide section of the navigation. The warehouses, one of which was built over the canal, have all been demolished leaving only a square basin. After crossing the Dove on a long brick aqueduct, the first of the wide locks is reached at Stenson. This is very deep and great care should be taken by boats coming up in it, for there are ground and gate paddles and the water tends to draw the boat forwards. The remaining five wide locks are not so deep as Stenson but all have the similar effect of drawing the boat. Going down the locks is easy, for there is no problem with the water as it flows out.

The village of Shardlow lies a mile from the junction with the Trent, and this is a place that must be explored. The A6 main road cuts through it, crossing the Trent at Cavendish Bridge, but the eighteenth-century village lies beside the canal. There are splendid warehouses, fine mansions where millers, maltsters and fleet owners lived, and smaller but equally gracious houses for their managers. An ancient boat-yard is now given over to pleasure craft, and fine old inns have their own moorings. The village was a vitally important interchange port, to which Humber keels sailed up from Hull to offload their cargoes which were then carried by narrow-boat to all parts of the canal network. One of the huge flour mills has been converted into an attractive museum, with a restaurant and shop and a trip-boat which runs through the village.

The canal finally enters the Trent at what appears to be a crossroads of navigations. The wide Trent lies straight ahead, having come in from the right beneath a towpath bridge. This section is navigable as far as Cavendish Bridge where there is a marina and British Waterways workshops. The River Derwent comes in from the opposite side to complete the cross. This was once made navigable as far as Derby but the navigation fell into disuse when the Derby Canal was opened. Now that, too, is no more.

The Leeds & Liverpool Canal
History
The line of a canal from Leeds to Liverpool across the Pennines, the backbone of England, was first surveyed by James Brindley but he had no further association with it. An Act of Parliament was obtained in 1770 but such were the problems to be faced that it was not completed until 1816 and not linked with the docks and the Mersey until 1846. Work was started at both ends and the limestones of Skipton were

being carried down to Leeds in 1777. Wigan and its coalfield were linked with Liverpool in 1775 but all the money was used up and the work was stopped. The original route was planned to make use of the Ribble valley as well as that of the Aire but this would have avoided the cotton towns of Chorley, Blackburn and Burnley where the canal was most needed. A change of route to include these towns brought in more money and work restarted in 1790. The original line would have avoided tunnelling but the change meant the need for tunnels at both Foulridge and Burnley.

In 1792, the Lancaster Canal was planned to run from Kendal to Preston and across the Ribble estuary to extend southwards as far as the outskirts of Wigan. This southern section would have run parallel to the projected line of the Leeds & Liverpool and it was therefore decided to bring the latter canal down seven locks at Wheelton to join the Lancaster Canal. Both navigations were built to the same width and the southern section of the Lancaster kept to one level. At Aspull, the Leeds & Liverpool drops down twenty-three more locks to join up with the earliest section.

The route

Cruising the canal from Liverpool to Leeds, the boater may possibly have crossed the Mersey from Ellesmere Port and Eastham. The Boat Museum Trust has taken several boats through this way but arrangements must be made with the Ship Canal Company, the Mersey Docks Board and the British Waterways Board for the Stanley locks. The trip is interesting but should only be made with other boats and, if possible, with a Mersey pilot and care must be taken that the tides are suitable. At spring tide, the water races through the narrowed channel between Liverpool and Birkenhead and the trip is not advised for the timid or the foolhardy!

Stanley dock and the four locks were opened in 1846 and the dock itself is surrounded by fine warehouses. The locks are large and are separated by short, wide pounds. Turning left at the top, the canal runs on a level for 28 miles, the first five through the heavily built-up area of Liverpool, Bootle and Litherland. Aintree racecourse is then passed and people tell me that they have had a splendid view of the Canal Turn from the cabin roof.

From here onwards, the scenery is more rural and the first swing bridges are met. Many canals have some special feature which impresses itself on the mind and which is remembered long after the cruise is finished. On this navigation it is the numerous swing bridges, with as many as 19 in the 17-mile Skipton pound. The drill is to put a crew member ashore, preferably with a bicycle, to reach the bridge, check that there is no traffic about to cross and shift the bridge. We found that practically all the bridges swung easily and there are often young helpers only too ready to push. We also found that extra care was then needed or the bridge was swung so fast that it bumped its buffer and started to close again, much to the alarm of the steerer. The bridge must be swung back again for road traffic after the boat has gone through, and the crew member can then be taken aboard or can go on to the next bridge. The towpaths are excellent and well maintained and the canal is deep enough for the average pleasure boat to cruise up to them without going aground.

The canal comes within a few miles of Southport at Scarisbrick and coaches used once to meet the packet boat at the bridge. Burscough is an attractive canalside village. Ainscough's huge mill was the last in this area to use canal transport and the British Waterways workshops are housed in a small group of fine eighteenth-century buildings. The actual junction with the Rufford branch is also attractive, with its bridge dated 1816, its drydock and surrounding cottages and the Ship Inn.

From Burscough the canal crosses the Douglas and continues along the north side of the valley to the pretty village of Parbold. It then begins to climb through four well-spaced locks to the outskirts of Wigan. When first built, the locks were short, for there was no connection with the rest of the canal system and the expected craft were the short, beamy West Country keels of Yorkshire and the slightly longer but slimmer Mersey flats. When the link was made with the Bridgewater in 1820 – with the opening of the branch from Wigan to Leigh – the locks from Wigan to Liverpool were lengthened so that Bridgewater barges and pairs of narrowboats could use them. The locks above Wigan were left unaltered and full-length narrowboats cannot take this route over the top.

Wigan is famous for its pier and for its massive flight of 21 locks which lift the waterway out of the coalfield into open country. The pier is a small, raised portion of the towpath where cargoes could be tipped into waiting barges but it was made famous by the Lancashire comedian, George Formby senior. The locks are hard work but there is great satisfaction in reaching the top, especially as there is a canalside inn adjoining each of the three top locks! The paddle gear is padlocked but a special key can be obtained from the British Waterways offices in Wigan. The actual paddle gear of the Leeds & Liverpool Canal is of great interest on account of its variety. There are the cloughs, pronounced to rhyme with cows, wooden beams that you lift up to uncover the sluice. There are ground paddles operated by worm gearing and there are gate paddles that slide horizontally. Some of the paddle gear has fixed handles and on some you use your own windlass, while others are so stiff that you are recommended to acquire and use a special long-handled windlass.

Chorley, Blackburn and Burnley are passed as the canal wends its way through industrial Lancashire but there is a surprising amount of open country, with views across to Pendle Hill. Much of the land is high with deep valleys and the canal keeps to two levels separated by the six Blackburn locks. Because of this, the channel winds a great deal, making sharp curves and doubling back upon itself. In Blackburn there is a notable embankment at Ewood and at Burnley there is the even higher and longer embankment – the straight mile. Boaters cruising along here have long views across the town and the embankment is so high that many Burnley people seem unaware that they have a canal in their town. Gannow tunnel, on the south side of the town, is a wide stone-arched structure without a towpath and is a little over 500yd long.

Beyond Nelson, the canal rises through the seven Barrowford locks to the summit pound and continues through the beautiful Craven countryside for most of the rest of its course. It dives into Foulridge tunnel, a little short of a mile in length and also without a towpath, whose chief claim to fame is the cow which fell in at the southern end and swam right through to be revived at the pub at Foulridge. Rather sadly, this feat has been repeated more recently by another cow at Preston Brook tunnel, though the Foulridge cow had further to swim.

The Craven uplands are strikingly beautiful as the canal contours its way through them and many of the high hills rise from the northern slopes. Locks at Greenberfield, Bank Newton and Gargrave carry the waterway into the Aire valley and the river, still only a mountain stream, is crossed on the Priest Holme aqueduct. Skipton is the only town of any size along this section and the attractive little Springs branch comes in from the north, having run from beneath the castle right through the centre of the town. In the past, limestone from the very large quarries north of the town was loaded from chutes into barges waiting below. Boats over 35ft in length cannot wind in the small terminal basin and on our trip we had to come out backwards.

Kildwick is another village of outstanding beauty and the canal continues through Silsden to Bingley where the mighty staircase locks begin. When John Longbothom built this end of the canal he must have felt that the Pennines, with their heavy rainfall, would produce a limitless supply of water for most of his locks are grouped into staircases, which are very wasteful of water. Besides the Bingley 5 there are 4 staircases of 3 locks and 3 staircases of 2. Such structures are suitable for surmounting a steep incline but they have many disadvantages.

The Bingley 5-rise consists of 5 locks with 6 pairs of gates for the whole flight. If you reach the top lock with the intention of going down when a boat has just come up, you will find all the locks full. You can cruise straight into the top lock but you cannot empty it into the full lock below. You have to go to the bottom and empty that, and then empty the penultimate into the bottom and re-empty that, and continue until the four below you are all empty. Only then can the boat come down bringing a lockful of water with it. In like manner, ascending when all the locks are empty, the top four must be filled before proceeding. Fortunately, the lock-keeper is usually present and he makes sure that mistakes – such as flooding the towpath or completely emptying a lock – do not occur.

Two narrowboats can pass in a staircase and this is particularly easy in a two-rise lock. One enters a full top lock while the other enters the empty bottom lock. When all gates are closed, the paddles between the two are raised and a level is achieved. When the middle gates are opened, the two boats can pass. These locks are splendid structures but they are most wasteful of water and, in commercial days, wasteful of time.

Saltaire is an attractive industrial village built largely by Sir Titus Salt in the mid-nineteenth century. His mills on the canalside, the terraced houses for the operatives, the church and the school, all stone-built, form a complete entity. Rodley is on the outskirts of Leeds and much of the route from here is within built-up areas, though there are several places of interest before Leeds is reached. Kirkstall Abbey, one of the most complete of the late Norman Cistercian houses, is just across the valley and a visit is well worthwhile.

The monks' forge, a mile to the west, was expanded in the eighteenth century and grew steadily into a very large works. The Newlay and Forge locks, both staircases, stand beside it.

The canal finally locks down into the River Aire to complete its 127-mile journey. The area round Office lock is beautifully kept and forms a good mooring for exploration of the city. The Aire itself is a major navigation and for those prepared to cruise the tidal Trent, a circular route can be planned.

The Grand Union Canal
History
The Grand Union Canal is the most important main line in the country and has carried more commercial traffic than any other. It runs from London to Birmingham and was still heavily used up to and throughout the last war. Like so much of the canal system, its commercial activities have vanished and it is now a splendid waterway for pleasure cruising.

Unlike the two main lines already discussed, it was not built by a single company but was formed by the amalgamation of a number of separate canals, most of which were built during the period of the canal mania. The Oxford Canal, when completed in 1790, had provided a route from the Midlands to London via the Thames, but this river navigation was in a poor condition. In 1793, an Act of Parliament permitted the Grand Junction Canal Company to build a more direct route from the Oxford Canal at Braunston to Brentford on the tidal Thames west of London. The engineer was William Jessop. Two years later, the Paddington branch was authorised to bring the route nearer to London itself. This branch and the Regent's Canal are described on pp103–8. The Grand Junction Canal was built with wide locks, bridges and tunnels so that barges could be used but the two great tunnels of Blisworth and Braunston proved such a bottleneck that the company restricted traffic to narrowboats in 1815. The whole canal was open by 1800, except for Blisworth tunnel, which took five more years during which time a tramroad was laid over the top.

Though this line was of great value to much of the Midlands, it alone was insufficient for Birmingham traffic. This would still have had to take a long way round via the Birmingham & Fazeley and Coventry Canals, the 'bottom road' of the boat people (pp119–20). Thus in 1793 and 1794 two other Acts were passed, permitting the building of the Birmingham & Warwick and the Warwick & Napton Canals respectively. Though their bridges and the tunnel at Shrewley were built wide enough for barges, narrow locks were used to save water. Both canals were open by 1800 and there was then a direct route from Birmingham to London.

In 1929, the two Warwick canals were sold to the Regent's Canal Company and in the same year all three combined with the Grand Junction to form the Grand Union Canal. By this time powered boats were becoming more common and many boats were travelling in pairs. The wide locks were a great help, for the motor and butty could share a lock. Thus, during the high unemployment of the 1930s, government money was made available to replace the narrow locks of the Warwick canals with wide ones as far as Sampson Road Depot. Channels were also dredged, banks strengthened and the five miles of the Oxford Canal between Braunston and Napton were upgraded. This meant that the whole length of the Grand Union Canal from London to Birmingham was of barge width and in good condition.

The route
Starting from the Sampson Road Wharf in Birmingham, at the top of the narrow Camp Hill and Garrison locks which lead down to Salford junction, the line passes factories and large estates. Soon, however, it runs into more open country beyond Solihull to reach the first five wide locks at Knowle. This is an attractive and well-kept flight, built in the 1930s, and the earlier six narrow locks lie along the east side. They

81

now form bywashes though it seems a pity that they were not retained to save water, especially for pleasure boats. Kingswood junction is on the 9-mile pound below the locks and a link is made with the Stratford Canal. The wettest tunnel I know – Shrewley – comes next and we always advise good oilskins or a good umbrella! A horse path runs through its own little tunnel at a higher level and horse-drawn boats had to be legged through.

The great flight of locks at Hatton drops the canal down to Warwick in the Avon valley. On a bend below the first three locks are the British Waterways workshops and then lock after lock occurs for a full half-mile with splendid views over the town of Warwick. The paddle gear on the lockside is enclosed and each paddle takes 23 turns to raise or lower. If all locks are against the boater, 4 times 23 on each of 21 locks provides a lot of exercise. The boater is not allowed to moor for the night in the intervening pounds, so once started the whole flight must be worked. The canal used to run on into the town with the Saltisford arm but this has been disused for many years. It is pleasant to hear that it is now being dredged and restored, for Warwick makes very poor showing on the main canalside.

Warwick and Leamington are almost linked up, though the Avon runs between the two in a pleasant green valley. The canal crosses it on a sturdy, brick-arched aqueduct; it is here that it is suggested that a link could be made, perhaps by means of a boat lift. The higher Avon is a wide and deep river and would make delightful cruising. The spa town of Leamington is not seen to its best advantage from the canal and we were only too happy to cruise on into the open country beyond.

The twenty-three wide locks which lift the canal out of the Avon valley do not occur as a single flight but are well spaced out into smaller flights and single locks. Once more, the old narrow locks can be seen alongside. The 5-mile length of the Oxford Canal is reached at Napton junction and left again at

Braunston, a beautiful village on the hilltop, with its church and windmill (now without sails) dominating the scene. Two large boatyards are found on this stretch: the one with wide lakes is entered from an arm which was once the original line of the Oxford Canal, and the other from below the bottom lock. Six locks lift the canal to the second of its three summits and Braunston tunnel carries it through the Jurassic limestone and ironstone ridge. The tunnel is over a mile long and without a towpath, and it is wide enough for two narrow-beam boats to pass. The tunnel has a slight Z-bend near its eastern end, caused by mistakes made in its construction.

Norton junction with the Leicester line (p99) lies two miles beyond Braunston and a wide, straight stretch of the canal brings us to Buckby top lock. The A5 main road crosses just below the top lock and the wharf is the centre of a small community. It is possible to obtain a temporary licence and lock-key for the River Nene at the general store. The seven Buckby locks bring the canal parallel with both the M1 motorway and the main railway line from Euston. Cars and lorries rush by at breakneck speed on one side and trains travel even faster on the other. As we glide between at walking place, we are so thankful that we are using the older and quieter method of travel. After little more than a mile, the three lines of communication spread out a little and the canal dives into the silence of woodlands.

Gayton junction comes next from where a narrow branch canal drops down to Northampton and the River Nene (pp166–8). We then reach the great Blisworth tunnel, over 3,000yd long; it also has no towpath and is wide enough for two narrowboats to pass. Beyond it is the charming canal village of Stoke Bruerne with its attractive warehouse, now the British Waterways Museum, and its adjoining row of beautifully kept houses. Sister Mary, who was the boat people's trusted friend and medical adviser, lived in one of them. Opposite is the Boat Inn, with outside tables at which people can sit and enjoy the scene with its own special atmosphere. The village would hardly be found by road but by water it was an important night mooring for boaters.

The canal drops into the valley of the Great Ouse to cross the river on the cast-iron Wolverton aqueduct. This is far lower than that at Pontcysyllte (p64) and is twice the width but it still looks a long drop into the river below. There have been proposals to make the Great Ouse navigable from Bedford to this point and to effect a junction, possibly by a boat lift, but nothing has come of them. Those of us who love the Fen rivers would be delighted if one such scheme were to come to fruition.

The canal remains on a level for 15 miles, except for a very shallow lock at Bletchley which is said to have become necessary through a mistake in the levels when the canal was being dug. It then begins to climb again as the long line of the Chiltern scarp looms up in the distance. As this is approached, Ivinghoe Beacon stands out to the east and the Marsworth flight of locks, 'Maffers' as the boat people called it, lifts the canal to the Tring summit. The Aylesbury arm drops down through sixteen narrow and fairly shallow locks at Marsworth and the abandoned Wendover arm runs off westwards on a level from the summit at Bulbourne. The British Waterways workshops here occupy a noble group of buildings erected when the canal was cut.

The Tring summit runs nearly straight for 3 miles through a deep chalk cutting before beginning the long drop through 56 locks to the tidal Thames. A fine old inn stands on the main road near the top lock and both inn and lock are called Cowroast. We asked the origin of the name at the inn and were told that it was originally Cow Rest. The road, the canal, and later the railway, had all chosen the lowest gap through the Chilterns, a gap which had been used for many centuries before they came. It was through here that the cattle were driven onto the hills for summer pasture and back to the low ground for the winter. The drovers would rest for the night at the inn.

The railway is never far away for much of the rest of the journey and attractive towns have grown up on the wooded dip slopes of the hills, ideal for London commuters. Paper mills on this section used to get their coal by canal and this trade continued to Croxley Mill until the 1970s. Rickmansworth is well known to the canal folk for the building of generations of canal boats and it is here that the River Colne makes its first appearance. It enters and leaves the canal many times and watercress beds lie between river and canal.

The lock at Cowley Peachy, south of Uxbridge, brings the navigation onto a long pound. This was the first lock that the trainee boatwomen met in wartime and it is well described in the books by Susan Woolfitt, Emma Smith and Eily Gayford (see Bibliography). The 5-mile level Slough arm runs off to the west and the famous depot at Southall is 4 miles further on. Here the boats used to moor and wait for orders, perhaps to collect cargo for Birmingham at Brentford or Limehouse. Again this is beautifully described in the accounts of the boatwomen who trained and took over the boats in wartime. Bulls Bridge is here, with the Paddington arm extending through to the Regent's Canal and on to the Lee and Limehouse (pp155–6), while the main line continues southeastwards to Brentford. It drops through locks at Norwood and Hanwell to the extensive Brentford basin and then through two more locks to the Brent which links with the Thames opposite Kew Gardens.

The Grand Union Canal has always been a noble navigation and millions of tons of goods were once carried upon it. Perhaps it still has a commercial future, for boats use far less fuel than lorries. It is certainly a delightful route for the pleasure boater.

6

COUNTRY CANALS

All canals have rural stretches, even those that thread through the Black Country or the suburbs of London. There are some, however, which seem to avoid even the smallest villages as they thread their way through fields and woodlands. Though all were built for some particular purpose, such as the linking of a coalfield to expanding industry, their routes were largely governed by the lie of the land. For the boater, it is their remoteness which is their particular attraction for they present a picture of unchanged England as it has looked for many generations. Even the villages and hamlets along their courses are themselves off the beaten track and have remained unspoilt by modern developments.

Fortunately there are many such canals or lengths of canal in England, some well known to the boating fraternity and busy with cruisers during the summer months, but some much quieter. Even on the most heavily cruised waterways, the occasional locks and tunnels tend to concentrate the boats and, in the stretches between, it is possible to find solitude.

The Ashby Canal
History
The Ashby Canal was built to tap the coalfields on the Leicestershire–Warwickshire borders. It ran on one level

(*opposite top*) Middleport Pottery, Stoke-on-Trent. China clay from Cornwall used to be carried on the Trent & Mersey Canal by narrowboat; (*centre*) The Swan at Fradley junction, once a regular night mooring for boaters on the Trent & Mersey and Coventry Canals (*Harry Arnold*); (*bottom*) Wigan Pier on the Leeds & Liverpool Canal. Note the rails curved up as a buffer for trucks offloading into boats (*Ware Collection, National Waterways Museum*)

through this area to join the Coventry Canal at Bedworth, covering a distance of some 31 miles. There were numerous schemes to extend it northwards to link with the Trent & Mersey Canal at Burton but all were abortive. Tramways were laid to bring coal and limestone to its northern tip and mines were opened at Moira, Measham, Ashby and Swadlingcote close to the canal. So much coal was won from beneath the navigation that subsidence closed the top 9 miles and the canal now terminates in a field at Snarestone, south of the coalfield. It is perhaps best known for the Measham pottery, the so-called 'barge teapots'.

The route

The canal runs through rich farmland between the two towns of Nuneaton and Hinckley. Nuneaton lies out of sight, 2 miles to the west and Hinckley is reached by a short arm, but is otherwise invisible. The canal also passes the two villages of Shackerstone and Snarestone, both tiny and very charming. Snarestone can hardly be seen from the water, for it stands on a slight rise and the canal passes beneath it in a short tunnel.

The remoteness of the villages was brought home to us when we were in need of groceries. We moored at Shackerstone and walked a few hundred yards into the village. We asked a villager for directions and were sent to the post office, the only shop which, we were told, closed at midday. As it was a minute or two past by the church clock, we returned to the boat and pushed on to Snarestone where we made similar inquiries. Here the shop closed at 1pm and, as we were a few minutes late, we should have to make for Measham, 2 miles further on. A bus appeared and my sister caught it. I collected

(*opposite top*) Bingley Five-rise locks on the Leeds & Liverpool Canal *c*1912. The boat is being hauled out of the bottom lock by a horse which has its feeding bowl (*Ware Collection, National Waterways Museum*); (*centre*) Brentford basin and locks on the Grand Union Canal; (*bottom*) City Road locks on the Regent's Canal with Islington tunnel in the right background

bags from the boat, missed the bus and started to walk. The bus took a roundabout route through the neighbouring villages and the two of us reached Measham at the same moment!

The Ashby Canal can claim two important events which occurred along its route, even though both were before its time. The Battle of Bosworth – which ended the Wars of the Roses and placed Henry Tudor firmly on the throne – was fought on land alongside and it was at Gopsall Hall where Handel stayed to compose his great work, *Messiah*, completed in three weeks. The hall was demolished during the last war but the woodlands are exceedingly beautiful. There is a little wharf at Gopsall; when the last carriage of coal finished at Ilott Wharf further north coal was carried by lorry to Gopsall and loaded there. Sadly, no coal has been carried on the Ashby Canal for some years.

The Caldon Canal
History

The Caldon Canal can claim similar peace though it is a completely different type of navigation. Built early in the canal age, its purpose was not the carriage of coal but limestone from the great quarries of Cauldon Low (the spelling of the hill and the canal varies). Its further purpose was to carry water from reservoirs in the hills to feed the ever-busier Trent & Mersey Canal. It links with this canal above Etruria top lock and its first few miles beside the stripling Trent are urban. It still has limited commercial use, for just as Josiah Wedgwood realised that water carriage of fragile pottery cut down breakages, the present Johnson's Pottery, now part of the great Wedgwood concern, decided to link their works in Hanley and Milton by water transport. A shuttle service carries crates of pottery between the two on the 4-mile pound. Sadly, James Brindley's fatal illness is said to have started when he caught a chill surveying the Caldon which was then engineered by his brother-in-law, Hugh Henshall.

The route

The canal leaves the built-up area at the end of the pound beyond Milton and continues its course through rural scenery. It crosses the Trent, a few miles only from its source, and climbs through Stockton Brook to a summit pound a little short of 500ft above sea-level. After only a couple of miles, it divides at Hazelhurst and the main line steps gently down the Churnet valley to the terminus at Froghall.

A main road crossing the valley from Leek to Cheadle passes the village of Cheddleton and here an ancient mill, now restored, stands astride the river. Powered by two large undershot wheels, the mill ground corn in its early days, later flint for pottery glazes and finally titanium oxide for paint.

It is this Churnet valley that is so remote and beautiful. Crossed by few roads, none following down its length, it is explored by the boater and walker alone. The canal itself enters the river, which forms part of the navigation for more than a mile, and leaves it again at Consall Forge. For centuries, the whole valley was busy with industry: inferior iron ore was dug from its sides which when mixed with imported ore, was smelted for iron. Limestone was available for flux and the thick woodlands produced charcoal for fuel. Early in the last century, 2,000 men were said to work in the valley but the industry declined. The great forge at Consall ceased work before World War I and peace has now settled on the whole area. The trees have grown to maturity again and the explorer must search carefully for traces of the ore diggings. Limekilns stand beside the towpath like medieval ruins, and nothing is seen of the forge itself but the sluice gear that regulated the water to provide power for the tilt hammers.

Consall Forge itself is a charming spot. A little railway line runs down the valley and the platform of a tiny, disused station overhangs the canal. Occasional passenger trains used to run on this part of the North Staffordshire Railway, but these stopped some years ago. An active railway society at Cheddleton is busy restarting them. The Black Lion stands in an isolated position and we wondered how it receives its custom. In bygone days, the forge workers must have kept it busy but where did the customers come from now? There always seem to be plenty of them. The valley is actually crossed by a footpath which descends on one side by 198 steps and ascends the other by 202. These, no doubt, guarantee to sober up those on their way home.

Having left the river, the canal has still nearly three miles to go. It clings to the steep side of the wooded valley with the Churnet tumbling over the rocks below. There is one more lock at Flint Mill, with the mill, its wheel powered by water from the canal, standing beside it. The canal then continues down the valley past Bolton's copper works, which gave it its last commercial carrying trade during World War II. A few hundred yards beyond the low and narrow Froghall tunnel the terminal basins are reached, and the attractive warehouse is used as the base for a horse-drawn trip boat in which excellent meals are provided. The ground around the basin has been cleared by Staffordshire County Council and laid out as a picnic area.

Froghall was a little inland port and it is worth allowing sufficient time for a full exploration around it on foot. A small infilled branch, just before the final bridge, entered a lock whose stonework is clearly visible. This was the first lock of the Uttoxeter branch, opened in 1811 but closed only 36 years later when much of its course was occupied by a railway. The lock itself lowered boats into a wide basin equipped with additional wharves; this basin was kept in use until after the last war. It is still in water but it lies deep in woodlands and is heavily overgrown. The Churnet valley from Froghall southwards is as remote as its northern stretches, but now there is no canal to help the explorer.

There is much more of interest to be seen at Froghall, for the limestone quarries are still 3 miles away and at a level hundreds of feet above the canal. The link was made by a primitive, gravity-fed railway and traces of this can be found in the woodlands above. There were actually four different lines, each an improvement on the one before. The first two were constructed with flat iron rails and though there are still traces in the woods, they are not easy to find. The third line, with L-shaped rails, was designed by John Rennie and was in action by 1804. It was laid out in level stretches and inclined planes, the lowest two of which can still clearly be seen. The bottom one went straight up the hill from the basin to the flat ground level with the top of the limekilns, which lie on the west side. The second went steeply up the hill to the right and is now occupied by a footpath to Whiston.

The fourth line was built in 1849, using flat rails to a gauge of 3ft 6in. It took a much straighter route and was worked by cable and gravity. The best place to see it is where it crosses beneath the A52 Ashbourne road at a minor crossroads about a mile south.

Had we taken the right-hand turn at Hazelhurst, we should have followed the Leek branch, built in 1797 primarily to link with the large reservoir being constructed in the Rudyard valley. It was made navigable beyond the Rudyard feeder to Leek, but this last stretch was filled in by the short-sighted townspeople after the last war. The construction of the canal caused two major realignments of the locks on the main line. They were originally well separated as they stepped down the valley from the bridge midway between the Endon arm and Hazelhurst. As the top pound was extended, this flight of three locks was abandoned and replaced by a staircase which led off at the point where the canal turns sharply to cross the valley. These locks were wasteful of water and in 1843 the present Hazelhurst junction and locks were built. The lower canal had to pass beneath the upper and so the attractive white-painted Hazelhurst aqueduct was built.

Beyond the aqueduct, the canal continues to run along the side of the Churnet valley in what is one of the most beautiful stretches in the whole country. There is a wide leafy towpath on the lower side and great trees flank the slopes above, together with masses of rhododendrons which bloom in profusion. After a mile, the waterway swings round into a wide lake, to be faced on the opposite side by a hill spur through which runs a tunnel. A further half-mile, through the tunnel, brings it to its present terminus, with the Rudyard feeder coming in from the north. Ahead is a small aqueduct over the Churnet and the channel is filled from this point. The reservoir itself can be reached by a footpath.

Both these canals, the Caldon and the Ashby, can be cruised in a weekend but each deserves to have more time spent on its waters.

The Llangollen Canal
History
The Llangollen Canal, like the two waterways described above, reaches a terminus though plans were made for all three to be extended and to form through-routes. In the original Act of Parliament of 1793, the Ellesmere Canal was authorised to run from the Mersey at Netherpool to the Dee at Chester, then to continue across the Dee through the Flintshire coalfield and the iron-working towns of Wrexham and Ruabon. It was next intended to recross the Dee at Trefor and the Ceiriog at Chirk, and to continue southwards to reach the River Severn. Branches were to run south to Llanymynech, where there was limestone, and to Ellesmere and Whitchurch. For a variety of reasons, the Wrexham length was never built and the southern reaches were not extended beyond the tiny village of Weston Lullingfields. The eastern end from Whitchurch, however, was continued to join the Chester Canal at Hurleston, and the feeder from Trefor to the Dee at Llantisilio was made navigable to Llangollen. Thus a north–south industrial waterway finished up an east–west country canal and today we can only be grateful that this happened. When later the Ellesmere and Chester

Canals became linked, and were joined by the Birmingham & Liverpool Junction Canal to the Staffs & Worcs at Autherley, and to the Trent & Mersey at Middlewich, the whole concern became the Shropshire Union Railways and Canal Company, to be affectionately known as the Shroppie. The length of the Shroppie which we are considering here is normally thought of as the Llangollen Canal and extends from Hurleston junction to that lovely town.

The route
The Llangollen Canal is 46 miles long and is so beautiful that is should not be hurried through. Furthermore, it is very shallow in places and has a steady flow of water from the terminus, causing a slight current. This makes the trip up to Llangollen slower than the trip back. The Horseshoe Falls at Llantisilio maintain a level in the Dee, and some of the waters are measured and channelled into the canal to reach a reservoir at Hurleston. As this is an important water supplier to mid-Cheshire, boats must be very careful not to pollute the canal.

The pleasure cruiser turns west at Hurleston junction from the main line of the Shroppie and climbs up through four locks into a navigation which winds through peaceful countryside. As it passes Wrenbury and Whitchurch, it continues to climb through single locks until it reaches a flight of 6 at Grindley Brook, the top 3 forming a staircase. Attractive bascule (lift) bridges carry minor roads across the canal and these have to be raised for the boat to pass and lowered back into place. An arm of the canal once ran right into Whitchurch but this was abandoned and filled in some years ago. Now the shopkeepers regret the fact that the boaters pass by and the council is reconsidering how best to dig it out again. A further arm used to run eastwards to the village of Prees; now all but the last mile has also been filled in, though the present terminus is used by a boatyard.

The countryside changes entirely at this point and a long,

straight and deep channel runs through Whixall Moss, a huge area of peat which has been dug for centuries. The towpath here provides a good mooring for those who love isolation and the flowers, birds and butterflies of the moss are worth a study.

Beyond the moss is another complete change of scenery as the canal flows between the meres, the lakeland of Cheshire. Ellesmere itself takes its name from one of the largest of these lakes and is reached from the canal by a short navigable arm.

After Ellesmere the landscape changes once more and we soon realise that the waterway is heading towards the hills of the Borderland and the mountains of Wales. The canal forks at Welsh Frankton junction and the branch to the south drops down a series of locks on its way towards the Severn. There is another junction after half a mile from which the Llanymynech branch runs south–west to link with the Montgomeryshire Canal. It is this length, and its extension to Welshpool and Newtown, that is being restored. On a clear day, the peaks of the Breidden Hills and the western slopes of the Longmynd, the Stiperstones and Corndon are visible from the main junction.

Two more isolated locks lift the canal about 15ft before it turns north to cross the two deep valleys of the Ceiriog and the Dee. We are now in the foothills of the Welsh mountains. The mighty aqueducts themselves are described on p64 and tunnels cut through the ridge between the valleys. The Vale of Llangollen is famous throughout the land and the canal runs first along its south side, crosses at Pontcysyllte and then continues westwards along the navigable feeder. The valley is thickly wooded and is particularly beautiful in spring when the young leaves are a brilliant green, and also in the autumn when the colours change. The feeder is both shallow and narrow and there are places where two boats cannot pass. The moorings at Llangollen are limited but are so attractive, for the canal is still some 50ft above the river and they look out over the river itself and over the ancient bridge. The final

2 miles to the Horseshoe Falls have to be covered on foot for there is no place for turning even a small boat. The towpath passes a small warehouse where an exhibition tells the story of canals and a horse-drawn boat takes trips along the waterway. A little further is the field where the International Eisteddfod takes place each year. From here, the woodlands flank the cut and the sound of rippling water is always with us as the Dee tumbles over its rocky bed. The canal terminates at the meter house which stands astride the channel to measure the water flowing beneath. Beyond is the lovely curve of the Horseshoe Falls.

The Oxford Canal (southern section)
History
The Oxford is an early canal and has its own especial character. When canals were first built, their only competitors were the roads and – despite the improvements brought about by the Turnpike Trusts – these were mostly in poor shape. The carriage of heavy or bulky goods was difficult and expensive and the coming of canals solved this major problem. Until the commercial success of these navigations became assured, the money available for their construction was limited and canal engineers looked for the most economic methods of construction. Tunnels, cuttings, embankments and locks were more costly than level stretches and canals were therefore surveyed to follow the contours as far as possible. Many of the early waterways wind backwards and forwards, following up every minor valley and skirting every little hill so that their total length far exceeded the actual distance between their termini. This had the additional advantage to the canal company that the toll based on mileage was greater on the winding route than on the direct one. The original Oxford is a perfect example of a contour canal. The north Oxford was straightened later (p138) but the southern section remains as it was built.

Country canals

The route

This length leaves the Birmingham route at Napton and soon climbs onto its summit level by a spaced-out flight of nine locks. Napton windmill dominates the north-facing scarp of limestone and ironstone which runs through England from south-west to north. The Cotswolds and Edge Hill form the highest parts of this ridge but it continues in a north-easterly direction into Northamptonshire and then runs northwards into Lincolnshire and Yorkshire. The beautiful limestone villages of the Cotswolds and the browner ironstone buildings of Northamptonshire are characteristic of this part of the countryside.

The top pound of the Oxford Canal runs along the outer face of the scarp. Ten miles long, it is remote and isolated amongst the fields. In the early 1960s, there was still a little commercial carrying of coal to the gasworks at Banbury. We once met a commercial boat negotiating one of the tighter bends, so we purposely ran aground on the inside of the bend to give it as much room as possible. Even then it only just got round. The larger cruisers have the same problem today and their steerers have less experience!

The village of Wormleighton stands upon a hill above the waterway and this is well worth a visit if a suitable mooring can be found. Tiny, ancient and beautiful, the stone houses nestle amongst tall flowering chestnuts and other giants of the forest.

Eventually, the canal makes a turn to the south to cut through the escarpment at Fenny Compton, its lowest point. A tunnel was originally built here, only to be opened out later, though the channel is still very narrow. There is now a complete change of scenery, for the canal is on the dip slope of the rocks and the level drops gently down towards the Thames valley. A flight of locks brings the navigation alongside the River Cherwell which it crosses on a level in two places. The canal leaves the river in a strange, diamond-shaped lock, designed to maintain water levels.

The particular feature of the Oxford Canal is the lift bridge, which differs from the bascule bridges of the Llangollen, the Caldon and the Peak Forest Canals. It has two oblique balancing arms which must be pressed down to the ground to raise the platform, and held down until the boat is through. This is particularly important for we have seen bridges swaying up and down in a gusty wind and they are far too solid to chance a collision.

Cropredy is another village which must be visited. It stands beside a well-kept lock and is a picture-book village with its little streets, church and inn. It is hard to believe that it was the site of a battle in the Civil War.

The one large town along this stretch is Banbury where Tooley's, the famous boat builders, once worked. There used to be a large basin but this was filled in to build a bus station. The town has lost much in destroying these moorings, for people now prefer to stop and shop in the villages.

South of Banbury, the canal becomes less remote as it passes through the villages of Kirklington, Kidlington and Thrupp on the way to Oxford. The canal branches below Duke's lock and the short Duke's cut connects directly with the Thames above King's lock. The main line continues into Oxford, though the terminal basin was filled in to provide space for Nuffield College. Isis lock takes it down into a branch of the Thames and a further cut takes it into the main river.

The Grand Union (Leicester section)
History

The Leicester section of the Grand Union Canal was built at several different periods for the northern reaches include the Loughborough and Leicester Navigations. The rural lengths really start once the environs of Leicester are left behind and the canal climbs up through 24 wide locks to Market Harborough. The last section to be built was the old Grand Union Canal from Foxton to Watford that joined the Grand

Junction at Norton. It includes the Foxton and Watford locks and the 20-mile top pound and it is this that is as remote as any canal in England. It was built with wide tunnels and bridges but the locks are narrow. Had these been wide, the barge canals of the north and south of the country would have been linked.

The route

After entering the canal at Norton, near Long Buckby, it approaches and is crossed by both railway and M1 motorway and climbs between them through the 7 Watford locks, 4 of which comprise a staircase. Once it has left the motorway behind, it winds about through the heart of the Northamptonshire uplands. It pierces the high ridge of ironstone three times, first at Crick to lie on the outside of the scarp, then at Husbands Bosworth and finally at Saddington to drop into the Leicestershire plain. Saddington tunnel is known for its bats which hang upside down from the roof. The thought of these little creatures scares some people, but it need not do so for their flight is accurate and their 'radar' system of supersonic squeaks allows them to keep clear.

The 20-mile pound from Watford to Foxton was cut 50 years after the Oxford Canal but it is just as winding. Crick and Yelvertoft lie a little way from the canal, which makes a wide sweep round the latter. Husbands Bosworth stands squarely astride the canal but the waterway passes beneath it in a tunnel so that the boater might never know that it was there. There are very few places along the whole length where a deep-draught cruiser can moor and even fewer where such a boat can wind (turn round). The waterway stands well over 400ft above sea-level on the face of the scarp, and gaps in the hedges give a long view westwards over the Midland plain. The little Leicestershire villages are marked with church spires and the rich farmlands extend into the distance. August is a beautiful time to cruise this length, for then the corn is ripening to give a patchwork of colour.

The village of Welford is at the terminus of a mile-long branch which runs along the north side of the Avon valley. The river rises above Naseby and is dammed to form a reservoir which feeds the top pound of the canal. It then flows beneath a small aqueduct and continues on its way to Stratford and the Severn at Tewkesbury. At the top of the Welford arm, above a single little lock, are some attractive red-brick buildings and the terminus itself is used as a hire-boat base.

The length below the Foxton locks (p55) takes a 5½-mile course to Market Harborough, though the town is a little over half this distance by road. Once more the canal is shallow as well as winding but it passes through beautiful woodlands. The final mile runs past houses with long gardens and lawns sweeping down to the water and the terminal basin is occupied by a large firm of boat builders and hirers.

Market Harborough is a fine old market town on the upper waters of the River Welland, which flows eastwards to the Wash. It had originally been intended to continue the canal eastwards to cross the further divide to Northampton in the Nene valley but money ran out. Had this happened, we should not have had that peaceful top pound from Foxton to Norton, the perfect example of a country canal.

Both the southern section of the Oxford Canal and the line from Leicester southwards to Norton deserve a full week's cruising to themselves. There is peace on each and so much of interest to see.

7

URBAN CANALS

All canals run through some built-up areas, for their original purpose was the carriage of goods to the customers. The major canals run into or through large towns, but it is still true to say that most of their lengths lie amongst quiet, rural surroundings. There are a few canals, however, that are almost entirely urban. The Regent's Canal is one such, running from the Paddington branch of the Grand Union to the tidal Thames at Regent's Dock in Limehouse. The Erewash is another, as it creeps down the Erewash valley from Langley Mill, through the Derby and Nottingham coalfield to reach the Trent a few miles east of Nottingham. The most extensive of all urban canals is the Black Country network known as the Birmingham Canal Navigations.

Though most pleasure-boat people make for the quiet countryside, there is much to be said for the urban canals. With their nineteenth-century mills, their warehouses and wharves, they retain an atmosphere of the past when huge tonnages of goods flowed backwards and forwards along them. Today, they are quiet and peaceful but there are constant reminders of bygone days. The retired boatmen are still to be found at the canalside pubs or sitting on a lock beam or even watching critically from a bridge. For the pleasure boater in no hurry, the retired boatman may be persuaded to tell the story of his busy past and of the boats and cargoes that used to be seen on the cut. When planning to spend some time exploring an urban canal, it is as well to note where the modern estates lie for groups of children playing can be as mischievous here as anywhere else.

The Regent's Canal
History

When considering the Regent's Canal, we can include the length of the Grand Union from Bulls Bridge to Paddington, and the short Hertford Union Canal which links the Regent's Canal to the River Lee. The Paddington branch of the Grand Junction Canal (later to become the Grand Union Canal) was sanctioned by Act of Parliament in 1795 and completed in 1801. It extends for 13½ miles on the level and was built to bring the Grand Junction more closely into London itself. Wharves and warehouses were constructed at Paddington, which became an extremely busy centre.

In 1812, an Act was passed to permit the building of a canal eastwards from the Paddington branch to the tidal Thames at Limehouse, thus extending the canal network down to the main docks area of London. John Nash, the architect of Regent's Park and of the splendid surrounding terraces, was interested in this canal and became a director. It was he who persuaded the Prince Regent to allow his name to be used. Though it was less than 9 miles long, it was an extremely expensive undertaking, with its 12 pairs of locks and 2 tunnels. A second Act in 1816 was needed to raise more money and the canal company was the first to be able to take advantage of the government's plans to reduce unemployment after the Napoleonic wars. It received a loan of £200,000 and was then able to complete the navigation, which was finally opened in 1820 at a total cost of over £700,000! It was soon extremely successful, with several basins of which the largest and busiest was beside City Road. Later in the century – as its line passed close to or beneath the railway termini of Paddington, Marylebone, Euston, St Pancras and King's Cross – it was suggested that the canal would provide a suitable route for a railway. Fortunately this was never built. The Regent's Canal became part of the Grand Union Canal Company in 1929.

In 1824 Sir George Duckett obtained an Act to build the

Hertford Union Canal (Ducketts) one mile in length, from below the Old Ford locks on the Regent's Canal to the River Lee in Hackney. With its three locks, it was completed in 1830 and was sold to the Regent's Canal Company in 1857.

The route

Turning eastwards from Bulls Bridge, Southall, we pass beneath a wide brick bridge which carries the towpath. The first few miles are through residential suburbs and we found a quiet night mooring opposite Sudbury golf course, which lies on the side of Horsenden hill. Thereafter, the canal passes through a completely urban landscape, from the Kensal Green cemetery and Wormwood Scrubs prison to factories, some old and some recently built. Regrettably, the towpath is made up of gravel and we kept seeing newly erected buildings with every window broken. The stones are just the right size to provide small boys with ammunition, though recently the London Canals Consultative Committee has changed all this. Older buildings have their windows covered with steel mesh. Near Paddington, we passed tall flats and a large terrace of old houses built on a curve. Just before the junction is a wharf from where the narrowboat *Jason* and the zoo waterbuses take trips along the Regent's Canal; the Canaletto Gallery, housed in a narrowboat, is moored nearby. The British Waterways canal office stands by the junction; here boats were once gauged on entering and leaving the Regent's Canal. We called in and were told that the lock-keepers would look out for us as we cruised on through London. Ahead was Paddington Basin.

Turning sharply to the left, we entered the Regent's Canal and cruised through the beautiful area known as Little Venice. The canal is wide, with a central island, and stately Regency houses overlook the waterway. The canal then dives into the short, wide Maida Hill tunnel and passes close to Lord's cricket ground to run through the north side of London Zoo. Animals can be seen and their cries heard, even

(above) Cropredy lock on the south Oxford Canal, beautifully kept and ablaze with flowers; (below) Husbands Bosworth tunnel on the lonely top pound of the Leicester Grand Union Canal

though the canal lies well below ground-level. Macclesfield, or 'blow-up', bridge was rebuilt in the middle of the last century after it was destroyed by the tragic explosion of a boat carrying a gunpowder cargo. The cast-iron supporting columns were re-erected but the earlier tow-rope grooves are now on the inside.

The former Cumberland branch leading to Cumberland Basin, now filled in apart from the entrance, lies ahead and the canal makes another sharp turn to the left, towards the Camden Town locks. Above these is the water-based youth club started by Lord St Davids. When we were cruising through we were invited on board the headquarters barge and were most impressed with the whole organisation. Well-disciplined children, often from the poorest homes, were enjoying themselves in small craft and learning to be responsible citizens. This was clearly the answer to the gangs who broke the windows of the new buildings that we had seen earlier.

There is a lone lock at St Pancras, which seems to be isolated amongst railway sidings and warehouses, and this is followed by the much longer Islington tunnel. From the west, there is a slight bend so that it is impossible to see through until the boat has almost reached the entrance. As it is used by full-width barges, it is essential to have a clear passage before entering. Beyond the tunnel the locks start again though they are fairly well spaced out. As with the earlier locks, they are all in pairs and it was here that the lock-keeper took charge of us, motorcycling down the towpath to see us through each one. There is a lot of floating debris which could easily jam the gates; if this occurred the pound above could be lowered or even emptied. As the navigation

(*opposite top*) Trent lock where the Erewash Canal enters the river Trent; (*centre*) Galton Bridge over the BCN New Main Line *c*1910: this view is now largely obscured by the new Galton tunnel (*Ware Collection, National Waterways Museum*); (*bottom*) Gas Street Basin and Worcester Bar at the junction of the Birmingham and Worcester-Birmingham Canals

was well used by commercial traffic, the lock-keeper made sure that this did not happen and we had a splendid run through. He continued to supervise us through the Hertford Union Canal, which runs off to the left alongside the attractive Victoria Park and even checked up the time that we intended to return.

The whole trip – past factories, Little Venice, the zoo, the many commercial basins and Victoria Park – was well worthwhile and the lower part of the River Lee ahead is similarly an urban navigation (pp155–6). Had we not turned into the Hertford Union, we could have continued on through four more locks to Mile End and Limehouse where the Regent's Canal dock, now known as Limehouse basin, fronts the tidal Thames. At the right state of the tide, the Thames can be entered and the return trip to Brentford made through the heart of London. Nevertheless, it should not be attempted by inexperienced boaters; even those with plenty of experience should take advice beforehand and, if possible, make the trip accompanied by another boat.

The Erewash Canal
History
The Erewash Canal is also an urban navigation, even though it does not pass through any large town. It is an early canal, built between the years 1777 and 1779; it is just under 12 miles long with 14 wide locks and it eventually became part of the Grand Union Canal system.

The route
The canal is entered at Trent lock opposite the junction of the Trent with the Soar, an attractive spot with beautiful views to the south across the wide river. It runs through New Sawley and Long Eaton, which became famous for machine-made lace. The lace mills here, and further north, were built in the second half of the nineteenth century and are fine brick

buildings with decorated chimneys. As with so many mills, they depended on the canal for most of their needs: coal for the fires, water for the boilers and raw materials. The story of their origins dates back to the 1870s when the lace-mill owners of Nottingham were at cross-purposes with their workers' union. Non-union labour came in from the Erewash valley and several mill owners decided to move into this region. The Long Eaton population grew from less than 1,000 in the 1840s to over 13,000 in 1901, and the town prospered.

Sandiacre is the next village to the north and a magnificent lace mill stands beside the canal beyond the main road. Opposite the mill is a small open garden with moorings for boats, and the shops are just across the way. Sandiacre lock is south of the village and the lock-house now belongs to a very active canal-preservation society. Above the lock is a canal junction from where the now-abandoned Derby Canal runs off to the south-west.

East of Sandiacre is Stapleford, which is separated from the canal by railway sidings. We nearly moored here for the night but were warned at the time that the sidings were marshalling yards where shunting continued throughout the night. North of this, beyond the high bridge which carries the M1 motorway across the navigation, are the extensive remains of the Stanton and Staveley ironworks. When we made our first trip in 1971, these were still in full operation, but 10 years later they were practically deserted.

Ilkeston comes next, strung out along the canal over a distance of 3 miles. The west bank is built up for most of the way but the towpath on the east bank runs close to the river valley. A disused railway strides across the whole valley on an impressive viaduct. Beyond Ilkeston, the canal crosses into Nottinghamshire by means of a small stone aqueduct over the river; it then runs through more open country, though Eastwood lies a short distance only to the east.

The terminus is the Great Northern basin at Langley Mill

and this has recently been dug out and restored to form an attractive mooring. The abandoned Nottingham Canal enters here, having run for approximately six miles parallel to the Erewash on the opposite side of the valley, before turning south-east to Nottingham.

Yet a third canal enters the Great Northern basin, this time from the north. This is the Cromford Canal, which tapped the coalfield further north at Pinxton and then swung west to pierce by means of Butterley tunnel the watershed between the valleys of the Erewash and the Derwent. Sadly, this canal has also been abandoned and filled in at its southern end. The Derwent-valley section from Cromford is being restored but the great tunnel has long since subsided and is unlikely to be reopened. Having passed the entrances of so many abandoned canals, we can only be thankful that the Erewash was saved and this was mostly due to the enthusiasm of volunteers.

So the short Erewash Canal, running through small industrial towns and lace-making villages, and with coal mines not far away, has much to attract the pleasure cruiser. Many of the little houses with gardens running down to the water's edge have made a feature of their canal environment and white waterlilies grow in the shallows. The people are friendly, the numerous canalside inns are welcoming, and the great lace mills with their splendid chimneys are a pleasant sight to see.

The Birmingham Canal Navigations
History: Old and New Main Lines
To some people, the idea of cruising through the Black Country is an anathema, while to others a canal holiday which did not include some section of the BCN would be unthinkable. A hundred miles of cruisable waters make up this system and a further 60, now abandoned, are still available to the towpath walker. They include some of the most

ancient of the English canals as well as some of the last to be
built. They are full of interest to the industrial archaeologist
yet they also include peaceful corners of green countryside.
They lie between factories, warehouses and estates and
wander peacefully beneath roaring motorways. We would
not want to spend our entire holiday cruising them but are
always glad to include some length in our itinerary.

The BCN is a conglomeration of canals built by separate
companies at different times. Most of these amalgamated and
were eventually leased to the LNWR, though the Stourbridge Canal remained independent and the Stourbridge
Extension Canal (a feeder to the former) became attached to
the Great Western Railway. All passed to British Transport
Waterways in 1948. The first to be built, by an Act of Parliament of 1768, was the Birmingham Canal which was
planned to link that city with the Staffs & Worcs Canal below
Wolverhampton. James Brindley designed a winding waterway, hugging the contours where possible and reaching a
short summit level at Smethwick, a little below 500ft; it was
complete by 1772. It had an important branch to the coalfield
at Wednesbury, actually in use as early as 1769. The high
summit was wasteful of water so John Smeaton proposed to
lower it by 20ft, removing 6 locks (3 up and 3 down) and
running it through a cutting. This new line was completed in
1787 but there were still many improvements to come. In the
1820s, on the advice of Thomas Telford, the main line was
shortened by slicing through the contouring loops and
digging a much deeper cutting through Smethwick. A tunnel
shortened the line at Coseley and a long, straight embankment below Tipton carried the line direct to the equally
straight Smethwick cutting. This section is known as the
New Main Line, though the Old Main Line from Tipton
through Oldbury and Smeaton's section is still in use and is
much the more interesting route to cruise. Both lines are
wide and deep, though rubbish is often found near the
banks.

The route: Old and New Main Lines

The link with the Staffs & Worcs Canal was made at Aldersley junction, rather less than a mile south of Autherley junction where the Shroppie enters. Turning in at the former, the boater is faced with the 21 locks which climb onto the Wolverhampton level, 473ft above sea-level. Despite the high, uneven ground throughout the Black Country, this level is maintained by the main canal and its numerous branches for nearly 50 miles.

There is a pleasant little wharf with a row of cottages above Wolverhampton top lock, and we have often chosen this for a night mooring for it is very close to the shopping area. Until a few years ago, the spot was isolated from the noise of the city centre by tall buildings and a high wall, but sadly these have now gone and the land has been cleared and opened out. It is still pleasant but it has lost the feeling of remoteness and secrecy which made it so attractive. Cruising through towards Birmingham, the surroundings at first are highly industrial: factories and warehouses, some ancient and some modern. Coseley tunnel, built wide with towpaths on both sides, cuts through one of Brindley's great loops, the northern length of which has been retained as it leads to the British Waterways workshops at Bradley.

The Old and the New Main Lines divide at Tipton, south of the tunnel, the New dropping down the three Factory locks to the Birmingham level at 453ft above sea-level. This, like the higher level, extends for approximately 50 miles and includes lengths of the Dudley, the Worcester & Birmingham and the Stratford Canals.

We usually prefer to cruise the Old Main Line which runs through Dudley, Oldbury and Smethwick. A branch runs south-west to the long, low Dudley tunnel and a further branch from this enters the attractive Black Country Museum. Having chosen the Old route, there are three other points where it is possible to drop down onto the New Main Line. At Bradeshall, a short branch descends through three

112

locks, the first two forming a staircase. At Spon Lane, three of Brindley's original locks drop down to the west as they formed part of the early branch to the Wednesbury coalfield. The final link is at Smethwick, where a further three locks, built by Smeaton to replace Brindley's original three, head towards Birmingham. Brindley's locks have now been filled in but it is easy to locate their position,

The Old Main Line has a number of other features of interest, including the aqueduct over the branch that leads to Netherton tunnel and the Stewart aqueduct which carries the Old Main Line over the New. Between these is the short branch which climbs up six locks to Titford Pools, where National Boat rallies were held successfully in 1978 and 1982. The branch runs past the Langley Maltings, perhaps one of the most beautiful buildings in the Black Country. The M6 is carried directly over the navigation for about half a mile and it is a strange feeling to cruise between the tall concrete columns which support the busy modern highway. We prefer the older method of travel. Just before the Smethwick locks, the short Engine arm turns off south to cross the New Main Line on one of Telford's beautifully decorated iron aqueducts.

Compared with all these features, the New Main Line is straight and dull. At the western end it is mostly embanked, while the eastern section lies in the very deep Smethwick cutting. Here it is crossed by many bridges, including Telford's Galton bridge, a graceful iron structure similar to the two on the Severn at Holt Fleet and Tewkesbury. Near Birmingham, the straight line cuts through three of Brindley's original loops: Soho, Icknield Port and Oozells Street, all of which are still navigable. It then turns right at Farmers Bridge junction to pass under Broad Street, which used to have a church and shops above the canal. These, too, have disappeared but worse is to follow as we enter Gas Street basin. This basin, in the very centre of Birmingham, used to be another quiet oasis completely cut off from the busy world. Sadly, a number of the old buildings which surrounded it have been demolished and the whole basin has been opened out. Clearly there are very great problems in treating old and disused warehouses but their complete removal has destroyed a piece of canal history. There are still a number of permanently moored narrowboats where members of the boating community live, and some of the older houses have been made into attractive flats, but the atmosphere has vanished.

History: the Stourbridge and Dudley Canals
There is a great deal more to the BCN than a cruise through the middle on one or other main line. Shortly after the Birmingham Canal was completed, the towns on the southern stretches of the Black Country considered their needs for water communication. Separated from the Birmingham Canal by the high ridge of ground on which stand Dudley, Netherton and Rowley Regis, they needed their own links with the Staffs & Worcs Canal and the out-side world. In 1776, two Bills were sent to Parliament: one was for the Stourbridge Canal, running from the Staffs & Worcs at Stourton to the town of Stourbridge with a branch to Brierley Hill, Black Delph and the Fens; the other was to link with this and to run round Brierley Hill to Park Head, Dudley. Both were completed in three years and the latter, the Dudley Canal, was extended by the flight of Park Head locks and the long Dudley tunnel to join the Old Main Line at Tipton. Before the end of the century, there was a further extension from Park Head westwards to reach the Worcester & Birmingham Canal at Selly Oak. This also involved the cutting of a very long tunnel at Lapal. In the mid-nineteenth century, a second link with the Birmingham Canal, this time with the New Main Line, was made via the long, and much wider, Netherton tunnel.

The Stourbridge and Dudley Canals were of particular importance to the area, which has extensive coal mines and a number of important glassworks. The Dudley Canal became part of the BCN in 1846 but the Stourbridge Canal remained independent until nationalisation.

The route: the Stourbridge and Dudley Canals
Entering the Stourbridge Canal at Stourton junction, the boat rises through four locks to a 3-mile pound through some of the most attractive rural scenery imaginable. The may blossom was in flower on the first trip that we made and the whole length alongside the River Stour was scented. The canal crosses the Stour and reaches a junction beneath a red sandstone cliff, the right fork swinging south to Stourbridge and the left entering the lowest of the Stourbridge's sixteen locks. It is hard to believe that this is the so-called Black Country, for the rocks are deep red and everything around is a lush green. A few locks up from the bottom a short arm runs back to Stuart's glassworks at Amblecote, which is dominated by a splendid glass cone. In the days before electric furnaces the constituents of glass were fused in glass cones, comparable to the bottle kilns of the Potteries. As glass manufacture requires a higher temperature than that of pottery, the cone is a much higher structure. There are very few left in the country and this is a listed building carefully preserved by the Stuart Company.

The line to the coal mines of the Fens runs straight ahead from the junction above the top lock, while the main line swings round to the right. This runs through a historically important industrial region and on one occasion, when we were joined by Mr John Hemming, a retired boatman, we were shown the forge where the anchors of the *Queen Mary* were made and a chain shop which had produced chains for Nelson's *Victory*. Originally, there were glassworks all along this stretch of the canal. The Stourbridge and Dudley Canals join at Black Delph and the latter immediately climbs through a flight of eight locks. These are referred to locally as the 'nine', even though the middle seven were replaced by a new line of six as long ago as 1858. It is still possible to follow the original line and there are traces of the locks themselves. The flight with its bywashes tumbling over waterfalls is perhaps the most beautiful urban flight in the country. Extensive views stretch out over the green countryside of the Stour valley and near the top is a long, low building, once the stables where Mr Hemming's horse was kept. He told us that he would fetch it daily and meet the boats which had arrived by tug at the top lock. He and others would each take a boat down the locks and the Stourbridge sixteen, returning with an empty boat to the top. Recently, we were pleased to see that the stables have been fully restored.

The canal continues to a single lock at Blower's Green and to Park Head where three locks lift the level to 473ft. When we first cruised the Dudley Canal, the locks were derelict and it was said that a railway viaduct that crossed the canal was to be replaced by an embankment. If this had happened it would have cut off the southern entrance to the Dudley tunnel, which would probably have been abandoned. A keen local society took up the case and saved both locks and tunnel. It then transpired that the railway itself was about to be abandoned! British Waterways Board restored the locks and at Easter in 1973 there was a rally of boats at Park Head to celebrate TRAD – tunnel reopening at Dudley.

The passage through the tunnel is exciting. The hill on which Dudley stands is a limestone dome, with thick coal measures on its south flank which contain seams of hard black volcanic rock. Entering from the south, much of the tunnel is brick-lined except where the volcanic rocks are exposed. After a mile, the limestones are reached and here the tunnel is unlined. The limestones include two thick beds of freestone, a very pure limestone excellent for building, which have been quarried and then mined for centuries. The mining has created great caverns from which side canals run into other parts of the hill; boats were once used to bring out the stone. Because of rock falls, a new tunnel has been driven through to other larger caverns to enable visitors to see these underground sights.

The canal from below Park Head is now on the 453ft level as it swings round the side of Netherton Hill. It runs northeast once more to Windmill End and to the great tunnel of Netherton. This was first lighted by gas, and later by electricity, but now the boater depends on the headlamp to make the passage. Local youths often cycle down the towpath and try to frighten boaters with ghastly shrieks!

The turn to the south-east at Windmill End used to lead right through to the Worcester & Birmingham Canal at Selly Oak, but the long Lapal tunnel has been abandoned for many years owing to subsidence. The present terminus is beside Hawne basin, once a railway interchange but now a large marina. Before reaching the basin, the navigation runs through Gosty Hill tunnel and the Stewart & Lloyds steelworks. On our first visit, the firm had just finished carrying on the canal but still had a large boatyard with narrowboats, tugs, a slipway and a repair yard. It sold off its fleet of wooden boats some years ago and the Boat Museum acquired two. There was also a bay in the corner of the yard full of brand-new rudders!

History: the Wyrley & Essington Canal

Besides the central and southern routes across the Black Country, there is a northern route, much of which lies on the 473ft Wolverhampton level. Leaving the main line of the Birmingham Canal at Horsley Fields, it forms part of the original Wyrley & Essington Canal which was built between 1792 and 1795 to tap coalfields in that area. The canal was extended between 1794 and 1797 to run through Brownhills, down a great flight of thirty locks to Lichfield and on to join the Coventry Canal at Huddlesford junction. Many branches were built in the nineteenth century: some ran north towards Cannock and to Anglesey basin, to tap the extensive coalfield; others went south to Walsall, Daw End and Rushall to

117

link with the main network. The Rushall and Tame Valley Canals were amongst the last to be built in the mid-nineteenth century.

The route: the Wyrley & Essington Canal
The first few miles of the Wyrley & Essington Canal from Horsley Fields is through the heavily built-up industrial suburbs of Wolverhampton. The canal then runs beneath the M6 motorway and passes the British Waterways yard at Sneyd, where the original line used once to climb up into the coal-bearing hills, reaching a height of well over 500ft above sea-level. From here, the extension follows the winding contours through open and rather derelict land, much of it occupied by tinkers' caravans. This is not an area to choose for a night mooring. The Walsall branch drops down to the right and the Cannock extension runs north to Norton Canes, where three boat builders have their yards.

The canal swings north at Brownhills, and at Ogley junction the short Anglesey branch taps water from the Chasewater reservoir. This is a charming spot, in the quiet valley below the great bank of the reservoir itself. There are wide basins where the boats used to load coal until the end of the last war but all is now peaceful and rural. From the top of the bank, the scene is quite different as motorboats and water-skiers rush across the waters at rather different speeds from the canal boats below.

The run south from here through Aldridge to Daw End completes the length on the Wolverhampton level, and the nine locks at Rushall bring the boater into contact with large modern estates and high-rise flats. The Tame Valley Canal is entered at Rushall junction and its long, straight stretches running on embankments and cutting deeply through high ground are reminiscent of the southern length of the Shroppie. Like the Shroppie, this navigation was built in the railway age, when all thoughts of contouring were dropped. Eastwards, at Perry Barr, thirteen locks are well spaced out,

118

the top ones in pleasant, open country. As the boater drops down, the motorway is approached and, long before Salford junction, the canal lies beneath it. Salford junction itself is important since it links the Tame Valley with the Birmingham & Fazeley Canal and with the narrow, north-western end of the Grand Union Canal. The River Tame runs below it, beneath an aqueduct, and, towering above, are the several layers of motorway which make up Spaghetti junction! Cars are rushing along at 70mph while the quiet motor cruiser slips along at walking pace. Motorway repairs are always being made and it is doubtful if the road will last as long as the 200-year-old canal!

History: the Birmingham & Fazeley Canal

The Birmingham & Fazeley Canal is the last to be mentioned here for it is an important link on the east side of the Black Country. Known to the boaters as the 'Bottom Road' as they were routed round to Bedworth and Coventry to collect a return load, it was hated by all. It joins the Birmingham Canal at Farmers Bridge, quite close to Gas Street, and the surroundings here are a good example of the best modern treatment of an urban canal. Tall flats with lawns and suitable safety fences stand above the canal on one side, and there is a modern pub alongside restored eighteenth-century houses. The arm above the locks is perhaps the best night mooring in Birmingham. The canal itself was built between the years 1784 and 1789 and its engineer was John Smeaton.

The route: the Birmingham & Fazeley Canal

The Black Country stands on a wide area of high, undulating ground at the edges of which are long flights of locks. On this navigation, the thirteen Farmers Bridge locks are immediately followed by eleven more of the Aston flight. The top locks are so close together that side ponds were built alongside them. Though they are narrow locks, each with a fall of only 7ft, they were hated by the boat people, who had to bow-haul their butties the whole way down. Coming from London to Birmingham on the wide Grand Union, their butties had shared each lock with the motors. Here they had to be separated. They were said to be black with oil and coal dust and the wartime boat women (see titles by Woolfitt, Smith and Gayford in Bibliography) describe how the wet towrope, trailing on the towpath and dragging on the lockside, made their clothes and bodies black. In the nineteenth century, when boats went singly, each with a horse, this unpleasant work did not occur.

North of Salford junction the canal passes many large factories, including Fort Dunlop, and gradually leaves behind the great conurbation of Birmingham. It drops down three narrow locks at Minworth and twelve more at Curdworth, and is never far from the River Tame. It passes close to Drayton Manor Park and zoo, runs beneath the A5 Holyhead road, and joins the Coventry Canal at Fazeley near Tamworth. The junction has recently been landscaped with good moorings and the area immediately around is an excellent centre for shopping. In theory, the Birmingham & Fazeley Canal extends northwards from the junction for a further 5½ miles to Whittington Brook. The Coventry Canal Company had run out of money and the Birmingham & Fazeley and Trent & Mersey Companies agreed between them to build the length from Fazeley to Fradley. This was done, and the Trent & Mersey Company then sold its length to the Coventry Canal Company. However, the Birmingham & Fazeley Company would not relinquish its length and continued to take relatively high tolls on all through-traffic until nationalisation.

There are several other short lengths of the BCN worth exploring, notably through Walsall, and there is much to show to those who are interested in industrial history. With careful planning, there are many attractive places to moor for the night for those who propose to make a thorough exploration of the whole system.

8

HISTORIC CANALS

All canals have their historical links with the development of the areas through which they pass. Some were outstandingly successful while others were never able to fulfil the hopes of their supporters. I have chosen four to describe in this chapter though others considered elsewhere might well have appeared here.

The Bridgewater Canal
History
This navigation was built under a series of Acts. The first, in 1759, authorised the building of a canal from Worsley to Salford. Work had not long started when, in 1760, a second Act allowed its extension across the Irwell and into Manchester, with a branch to the main Chester road in Stretford. The canal's original purpose was the carriage of coal from the Duke of Bridgewater's Worsley mines and the first loads reached Manchester in 1763. In 1762 a third Act permitted the extension of the Stretford branch across the Mersey, to reach the estuary at a place called Hempstones, near Runcorn. Finally, the Trent & Mersey Act of 1766 contained a clause enabling the two canals to join, and the Bridgewater to move its western terminus to Runcorn itself. The whole canal was opened in 1776.

In 1799 a further branch was pushed westwards from Worsley to Leigh; this was later to be linked with the Leeds & Liverpool Canal, which opened a branch to Leigh in 1820. The Rochdale Canal was completed in 1804, joining the Manchester terminus of the Bridgewater. Thus what was started as a purely local navigation became an important through-route between the North West and the Midlands, and a competitor with the Mersey & Irwell Navigation for Manchester–Liverpool traffic. It carried very high tonnages throughout the nineteenth century.

The route
The whole canal is on one level now that the Runcorn locks have been abandoned, and is controlled by a Trust which issues its own licences, separate from those of the rest of the canal system. There is an arrangement between the Trust and the British Waterways Board to allow limited use of each other's navigations without taking out a separate licence. Those wishing to make use of this when cruising from the Board's waterways should contact the Trust at its Preston Brook Marina office.

Worsley Delph is almost a shrine for people who claim that this is where the English canal system started. The Delph is a quarry of brown, coal-measure sandstones which has a sheer face on its north side and a small peninsula running out from the centre, bounded on both sides by water channels. These two channels link with the famous underground canals which issue from the rock-face of the quarry. They coalesce and run under a road bridge to link with the main Bridge-water Canal at its junction with the Leigh arm.

Worsley Delph used to be full of mining boats (starva-tioners as they were called) but all but one have now been removed. This is moored along one side of the Delph and another is on show at the Boat Museum. They were con-structed very simply, pointed at both ends, with vertical sides and a flat bottom; the coal was carried in boxes. They were thus the forerunners of the narrowboats which became the commonest craft on the canal system.

The water that flows out into Worsley Delph is bright orange in colour. The coal-measure rocks contain a great deal of ochre – the hydrated oxide of iron, or rust – and this is

(*above*) Ellesmere Port, now the site of the National Waterways Museum, on the Shropshire Union Canal; (*below*) Worsley Packet House and steps on the Bridgewater Canal, where packet boats for Liverpool and Manchester moored.

continuously pouring out into the Bridgewater Canal. The main tunnel was still used for drainage purposes until recently and it was possible to obtain permission from the NCB to travel along it in one of the maintenance starvationers. This practice finished in the early 1970s and the water level is now such that it is impossible to get through.

Beside the main canal at its junction with the underground canals is a fine half-timbered building known as the Packet House. In front of it is a flight of steps down to the canal and here the packet boats would moor to take on passengers. They used to run regularly in the early days of the last century, eastwards to Manchester and westwards to Leigh, Wigan and Liverpool. A short distance along the main line is a boathouse with striped wooden doors where the Earl of Ellesmere's pleasure boat was kept. Pictures show this to have been a handsome horse-drawn craft with a coat of arms on the cabin front. The earl had postillions riding ahead on the towpath and the uniform of one of these is in the Boat Museum. The boat itself was later used as a director's inspection launch and survived well into this century. Sadly it was broken up soon after the last war. There is a boatyard and drydock a little further along the canal.

When first built, the canal was carried over the River Irwell on a fine, three-arched aqueduct, considered to be a great wonder at the time. It was said to be the first time that one navigation had been carried over another, with boats passing over boats. People also wondered how the water could be prevented from seeping away. When the water was first let in, it is said that Brindley was so concerned that he could not stay to watch. He had used the standard method of lining with puddled clay and it proved to be completely successful. Now the Bridgewater Canal crosses the lower navigation –

(*opposite top*) Above Tyrley top lock on the 'Shroppie'; (*centre*) the Bratch locks on the Staffs & Worcs Canal. The lock-keeper's house stands beside the top lock and the toll-house is by the bridge; (*bottom*) Stourport, the northern top basin with the locks to the left of the Clock Warehouse

which since 1894 has been the Manchester Ship Canal – on the Barton swing aqueduct.

The earlier stone aqueduct allowed sufficient clearance for the Mersey flats using the Irwell – they could lower their masts – but it was too low for the very much larger vessels which were to use the Ship Canal. Leader Williams's swing aqueduct, working on the same principle as his swing bridges, was built beside the venerable stone structure, which remained open for navigation until the swing aqueduct was complete. Its position can be judged by the direction of the canal on both sides, and its stone piers are visible on the north side.

The canal then runs up to Castlefields in Manchester, where a fine group of eighteenth-century warehouses once stood; many of these were demolished after 1945. In 1837 a link with the Irwell was made by means of a shallow flight of three locks at Hulme. In the early 1960s these were replaced by a single lock, to speed up the grain barges carrying from the docks to Kelloggs in Trafford Park. This traffic ceased in the late 1970s and a very high toll is now charged for the use of the lock, the only link between the Bridgewater and the Ship Canal. The Irwell itself is navigable into the heart of Manchester and the IWA holds cruises on this interesting and historic section.

The Stretford branch of the Bridgewater Canal leaves the main line at Waters Meeting, a lovely name for a rather dreary canal junction. The Stretford's extension crosses the Mersey and runs almost straight through the south-western suburbs of Manchester, finally leaving the built-up area beyond Altrincham. The beauty of the next length lies largely in its attractive villages, with Lymm, Walton and Grappenhall quite outstanding. The Chester road crosses the navigation on the London Road bridge at Stockton, near Warrington. This was an important point on the canal. Coaches brought travellers to await the packet boats, beds were available at the nearby inn and the warehouse in which their goods were stored still stands. The canal takes a long sweep south to Preston Brook before turning north again and a short branch runs south to join the Trent & Mersey Canal at the tunnel.

Preston Brook was a vitally important canal port for well over a century and a half. Barges and flats could reach this point from Liverpool and goods were offloaded into warehouses for onward transmission by narrowboat. A huge tonnage of china clay and flint reached the Potteries by this route and many loads of fine china found their way to distant parts of the world through this interchange port. Now all but two of the warehouses have been demolished and there are no cargoes to be stored. A large, well-run marina has been dug out nearby and hire boats line the main canal. A big modern estate has also appeared in what is now the eastern end of Runcorn New Town.

The canal terminates at Runcorn but used to drop down through two flights of locks to the Mersey estuary, and later the Ship Canal. Both these have now been abandoned and filled in. Originally there was a single flight of 10 locks in 5 staircase pairs, with a fine Georgian house standing beside the bottom locks. This was built for the Duke of Bridgewater and it is said that he watched their construction from its windows. The locks became so busy that a second flight was built in 1827 and a series of docks was constructed at the bottom. Sir George Head describes a passenger trip in 1835 when he came from Liverpool to Runcorn docks by paddle steamer. The passengers walked up the towpath to the packet boat waiting at the top while porters carried up the luggage. Owing to the lack of use, the early flight was abandoned at the end of the last war and the second flight went the same way in 1965. The docks are still busy with traffic on the Manchester Ship Canal. From the western end of the Bridgewater docks, the Runcorn & Weston Canal (opened in 1859) ran for a mile to link with the Weston docks and Weaver. This, too, was abandoned at the same time.

The Shropshire Union Canal

History

The 66 miles of this long and most beautiful waterway have had a chequered history. In the first period of canal building, a company was formed to build a canal from Middlewich to Chester, with a branch to Nantwich. Middlewich was an important salt town and the Dee was still navigable to the old port of Chester. However, the Trent & Mersey Canal Company wished to retain its monopoly of the carriage of salt from Middlewich, and it succeeded in inserting a clause into the 1772 authorising Act which prevented the Chester Canal from coming within 100yd of the London Road. This had the desired effect of cutting off the Chester from the salt-works which lined the Trent & Mersey Canal.

The Chester Canal Company then changed its plans and ran its main line to Nantwich. (Middlewich had to wait another 60 years for its branch; only then did the Trent & Mersey Company agree to a junction. The branch – and its vital 100yd single-lock link to the Trent & Mersey – was opened in 1833.) Nantwich was primarily a market town and a great centre for Cheshire cheese, but the carriage of cheese was hardly as profitable as the transport of salt and coal and the Chester Canal did not prosper. It had been built with barge locks, including a great staircase flight of five at Northgate, and there were acute problems of water supply at the start. In addition, the port of Chester was silting up and losing trade to Liverpool with its deep-water channel and its growing number of docks.

The Chester Canal was completed in 1779. In 1793, a separate canal company was formed at Ellesmere in Shropshire for the purpose of building a canal from the Mersey and Dee to the banks of the Severn below Shrewsbury (p94). Work was started on the Wirral line from the Mersey and a junction was made with the Chester Canal. Docks were built at Netherpool on the Mersey and in 1795 Ellesmere Port – the port of the Ellesmere Canal – came into being.

In the third great period of canal building, not merely was the link to Middlewich constructed, but an Act of 1826 permitted the building of the Birmingham & Liverpool Junction Canal. This was to run from Nantwich through to the Staffs & Worcs Canal at Autherley junction, Wolverhampton. Despite engineering difficulties it was successfully completed in 1835. The old Chester Canal had now become an integral part of a great canal system, with links from the sea to the Midlands and the Potteries. It had amalgamated with the Ellesmere Canal in 1813 and in 1846 the whole group of canals became the Shropshire Union Railways & Canal Company. For most of the rest of its life it came under the wing of the LNWR and later the LMS. Thus, a cruise of the length of the Shroppie – starting with the Wirral section of the Ellesmere Canal, built in the 1790s, continuing with the first-generation Chester Canal of the 1770s and finishing with the Birmingham & Liverpool Junction Canal, constructed at the beginning of the railway age – is a cross-section of English canal history.

The route
Turning from the Staffs & Worcs Canal at Autherley, the boater cruises under a beautiful roving bridge, built on a skew, and enters a narrow stoplock. Thomas Telford, who planned this canal, was never a believer in railways. He was the last great canal and road builder but he realised that railways were going to become the canals' competitors for the carriage of goods. He therefore designed the canal to run as straight as possible, though this meant the construction of high embankments and deep cuttings. He also grouped his locks wherever possible, so that little time would be wasted. The long, straight stretches of canal are the most obvious feature and very soon the cuttings and embankments begin.

Before reaching the single lock at Wheaton Aston, the canal crosses the equally straight Holyhead road on the cast-iron Stretton aqueduct, so typical of Telford. Before

Norbury, the canal runs along the top of the great curving Shelmore embankment, 60ft high and over a mile in length. Rolt describes in *Thomas Telford* the problems that were faced in the construction of this bank. It subsided many times and was not satisfactorily completed, and water allowed in, until some months after Telford's death. Trees were planted on its sloping banks to consolidate the soil and these have now grown to be forest giants. They are so thick and high on both sides that a cruise along Shelmore's length is more like being in a cutting. There are beautiful views in the gaps between the trees, for the tall peak of the Wrekin stands up out of the Shropshire Plain to the south-west with the higher hills of the Welsh Borderland forming a backcloth.

Norbury junction is an attractive place, with the British Waterways workshops housed in buildings as old and gracious as the canal itself. There is a major boatyard, where hire craft are available and a pleasant inn on the bank above the towpath. A branch, abandoned in 1944, ran southwards from the junction, dropping down a long flight of locks to Newport and continuing to join the Shrewsbury Canal at Wappenshall. The loss of this beautiful waterway is much regretted.

The canal runs through the first of the really deep cuttings north of Norbury. Well over a mile long, its high steep banks are tree-clad and clematis hangs down from the branches which almost meet overhead. The whole atmosphere is more like a jungle than the heart of Staffordshire. It is particularly beautiful in the spring when the sun is out and the primroses are in bloom, but it is dark and sinister on a rainy day. The Shebdon embankment soon follows and a few miles further north is the equally long and even narrower Woodseaves cutting. Once through this cutting, and down the five Tyrley locks, the major cuttings are left behind though there are still a number less deep. During the canal's construction, the material from the cuttings was transported to the valleys to help build up the embankments.

The centre of Market Drayton is some little way to the west of the canal below Tyrley locks. As its name implies, it is an attractive market town and is well worth a visit. Further north the canal drops down the five Adderley locks, so beautifully kept that the lock-keeper has won several national prizes. A mile beyond are the fifteen Audlem locks which drop the navigation into the Weaver valley and the Cheshire Plain. Audlem itself is a delightful little town and we always stop for shopping there since every shop is within a few hundred yards of the mooring.

Further straight lengths, with two locks at Hack Green, bring the canal onto the long embankment at Nantwich, which was only built because the owner of Dorfold Hall refused to allow the navigation to take a more logical route through his land. It then runs beneath a bridge to join the older and wider Chester Canal close to Nantwich basin. The Chester is a very typical early navigation, winding about on the contour. Its greater width shows that it was constructed for barges.

Two important junctions lie north of Nantwich, the first at Hurleston where the Llangollen branch comes in from the west, and the second at Barbridge, from where the Middlewich branch runs eastwards to join the Trent & Mersey Canal.

To reach Chester, the canal had to breach the long escarpment of hard Keuper sandstone which forms the Bickerton and Peckforton Hills on the west and Delamere Forest and Helsby and Frodsham Hills on the east. To do this, it made use of the gap cut by the little River Gowy and for a spell river, canal, railway and road are all close neighbours. The waterway drops down a series of wide locks, starting with the two-lock staircase at Bunbury with the old stables alongside. These date back to the days of the packet and fly boats, when regular changes of horses were needed. Away to the left is the pointed outlier of Beeston Hill, dominated by the ruined Norman castle. It is worth mooring by Wharton lock

131

and taking the footpath across the fields to the road and the gatehouse. It is then a long, steep climb to the castle walls but the views over the Cheshire Plain and into Wales are superb. The gleaming ribbon of silver far below marks the line of the canal.

The navigation from this point to Christleton is perhaps the least attractive pound, for it passes near the bleak Rowton Moor where King Charles I's soldiers lost that vital battle. Five well-spaced locks at Christleton drop the canal into Chester.

The best mooring for shopping and for exploring Chester is on the wharf by Cow Lane bridge, but the most exciting length of the canal is still ahead. Beyond the bridge the great medieval walls of Chester rest on Roman foundations. They tower above the navigation, which actually follows the line of the Roman moat, and the busy Northgate bridge crosses high above. The staircase flight of the three Northgate locks is at the end of the pound and the locks are cut out of the red sandstone. The whole flight is impressive and one realises how much more formidable it must have been originally, when there were five locks in the staircase. They were first built at almost exactly the same time as the Bingley five-rise on the Leeds & Liverpool Canal.

Below the locks, the canal takes a sharp turn to the right and enters the real canal port of Chester. Tower wharf on the offside is now a British Waterways yard but in bygone days it was the departure point for the Chester Packet, the horse-drawn passenger boat which ran through to Ellesmere Port. A warehouse with an arched, under-cover mooring stands behind the wharf and the fine, Georgian building adjoining it was once a hotel. People would arrive by coach and stay the night before travelling by packet to Ellesmere Port and on from there to Liverpool en route for America. A large covered drydock stands between the canal and the branch down to the River Dee and it is large enough to hold two narrowboats side by side. It used to belong to the canal company's boatyard, where its own fleet of boats was built and maintained. The boatyard is now privately owned but it still carries on the old traditions.

The last 8 miles to Ellesmere Port are through the rural Backford gap, a wide, glacial-overflow channel cut by melting waters at the conclusion of the last Ice Age. The final 2 miles are past the Stanlow oil terminal; the port itself is then reached.

Ellesmere Port is a fitting climax to a cruise along the Shroppie, for it houses the Boat Museum, now properly entitled the National Waterways Museum. It tells the whole story of the canals: their building, their use, their cargoes, and the people who worked on them. It has set out to collect, restore and maintain and to use the significant boats of the inland-waterways system. The collection includes narrow-boats, barges, tugs and dredgers and larger craft from rivers and estuaries. At the time of writing, some sixty different boats can be seen.

The port itself has an interesting history. It was opened in 1795 with a flight of locks to the Mersey, a dock and a few buildings which included offices and tollhouse and some stables. These, fully restored, stand today. When it became clear that the canal was to be linked to both the Midlands and the Potteries, Telford was asked to advise on a much larger layout. He did not live to see his work completed, but it included the basins seen today and several warehouses, the largest of which were destroyed by fire in 1970. Hydraulic machinery was introduced in the 1870s, complete with a pumphouse and boilers. The pumping engines are being restored and two of them are regularly steamed. The Manchester Ship Canal reached Ellesmere Port in 1891, after which ships could enter and leave the basins at any state of the tide. The little lighthouse still stands by the dock entrance, though it is no longer needed.

The canal port was busy until 1945, but it is now the container cranes of the Ship Canal's north wharf which have taken over. In its heyday, the warehouses would have been full of goods brought by sea awaiting narrowboat transport to the interior of the country. The associated workshops, repair yards, drydock and slipway can all be seen today. The fine buildings that still stand have been restored and form part of the Boat Museum.

Thus the Shroppie presents a picture of the whole canal age, even to its links with the Ship Canal.

The Staffordshire & Worcestershire Canal
History
The Staffs & Worcs Canal is 46 miles long from its junction with the Trent & Mersey at Great Haywood to the River Severn at Stourport. Started in 1766, it was completed and open throughout its length 6 years later. Compton lock, near Wolverhampton, is said to have been the first lock that Brindley constructed. Though it passes very close to the western edge of the Black Country, it is a wonderfully rural waterway and one of the most attractive of all cruising canals. Unlike so many of the narrow canals, its company remained independent throughout its long life until taken into the national network in 1948; like other early canals, it was highly profitable. It has many features of historic importance, including the port of Stourport built by Brindley after the town of Bewdley is said to have refused to become the terminus of the 'stinking ditch'.

The route
Starting from the Trent & Mersey, the canal is entered beneath a wide towpath bridge and crosses the River Trent and a mill stream on two small aqueducts. Beside the towpath is a little neo-Gothic tollhouse, recently restored and used as a canal shop. Half a mile further on, the navigation enters Tixall Wide, one of the most beautiful reaches of any canal in the country. The waterway widens into a lake nearly a mile in length and over 100yd wide, the whole held up by a

high bank – which carries the towpath – on the south side. The opposite side is shallow, with stretches of great reed grass in which nest grebes, coots, moorhens and other water fowl. Countless starlings appear at eventide and literally fall out of the sky to roost among the reeds for the night. On the hill above stands the gaunt gatehouse of Tixall Hall, though the hall itself has been demolished. Thomas Clifford, its owner, was prepared to allow the canal to be built provided that it did not spoil his view and this is the reason for the construction of the wide. The wooded hills of Cannock Chase rise up across the River Sow.

The canal crosses and then follows the Sow and its tributary, the Penk, missing Stafford by about a mile. A short branch, now filled in, actually locked down into the river which was dredged out and made navigable into the centre of the town.

The canal is then lifted up the Penk valley by a steady series of locks to flow past Penkridge to a summit at Gailey. This length used to be quiet and peaceful but the M6 motorway now lies close to it for about five miles and the roar of traffic is never far away. The Holyhead road crosses the canal just below Gailey lock and the towpath is carried beneath it in a small tunnel. Gailey is notable for its beautiful round-house built, it was said, to enable the lock-keeper to keep a lookout for packet and fly boats. As the boatmen of the latter carried whips which could be cracked like a pistol shot, and the former carried a post horn, it is unlikely that the lock-keeper would need to keep a watch. On the opposite side of the canal is an attractive tollhouse.

The top pound is 9 miles long and, in the environs of Wolverhampton, it passes two important junctions. The Shroppie runs off to the north-west at Autherley (pp128–34), and the twenty-one Wolverhampton locks climb up to the south-east at Aldersley (pp110–14). Though the waterway runs through the built-up area between Wolverhampton and its neighbour, Tettenhall, it remains mostly in cuttings and therefore little is seen of either town in this industrial area.

The River Stour's tributary, the Smestow brook, rises near Tettenhall and the navigation follows the valley all the way to the Severn. There are enough locks to make the trip interesting, though they are mostly spaced well apart. The Bratch is the most attractive flight with three locks spaced so close together that they look like a staircase. In high season, they form a bottleneck but the country above and below is so pretty that the boater should never grudge the waiting time.

Below the Bratch, the canal follows the beautiful wooded valley with red sandstone cuttings and two very short tunnels. The Stourbridge Canal comes in at Stourton junction and the navigation runs through the centre of Kidderminster, with fine carpet warehouses below the lock. Stourport and the Severn are now only 4 miles away.

Like Ellesmere Port, Stourport was built for the interchange of goods. Narrowboats brought their cargoes to its basins and warehouses, and the Severn trows carried them away to the port of Bristol, or even further afield. When Brindley planned the canal, the present site of Stourport was occupied by the small village of Mitton, a mile or so above the confluence of the Stour and the Severn. The actual confluence is surrounded by low ground liable to flooding; Mitton stood slightly higher and was therefore more suitable for development, since the Severn in flood has been known to rise by as much as 20ft. A basin was built with two wide locks down into the Severn: these are 76ft long by nearly 16ft wide, large enough for the largest trows afloat at the time.

Langford (see Bibliography) gives a full account of the Stourport basins and their steady development. In all, 6 basins were constructed: 4 at the higher level and 2 at the level between the 2 locks, though the 2 furthest west were filled in, as were drydocks which ran out from the upper one. The canal drops down into the corner of the largest and oldest of the four remaining basins. This has a fine warehouse with a clock tower on one side, and a second warehouse which now houses the offices and maintenance depot of the British Waterways Board. Next to this is the large Tontine hotel, a magnificent eighteenth-century building fronting the Severn, with gardens laid out on the slopes. It was important in the early days for passengers en route to Bristol and perhaps America; it is comparable with the hotel building above Tower wharf in Chester. Furthermore, it was a meeting-place for merchants, supervising the transfer of their goods.

The barge locks are not bridged and sailing trows could lock into the two upper basins without lowering their masts. These two locks, with a total rise of 29ft, were very wasteful of water when used by a single narrowboat locking down into the river. Thus in 1781 two staircases were added, each consisting of two narrow locks: one between the upper and lower western basin, and the other from there to the river. The angle between the two staircases is such that it makes it quite a difficult turn for a full-length narrowboat.

This fine interchange port is worth a lengthy visit by boat or by car, for there is still much to see of the fine eighteenth-century engineering and buildings. It was very busy with commercial traffic throughout its first 150 years but it has now been given over entirely to pleasure craft. Many sea-going vessels winter here and there is a boatyard in the upper basin. The lock-keeper will always advise visitors proposing to cruise the Severn, and all narrow-beam craft now use the narrow locks.

The Coventry Canal and the Oxford Canal (northern section)
History
These two navigations were both built in the early part of the canal era, forming the southern leg of Brindley's Grand Cross. The Coventry Canal Company ran out of money when it had opened the long level pound to Atherstone. It was with difficulty that it was persuaded to extend to Fazeley

and this was only agreed after the Birmingham & Fazeley and Trent & Mersey Canal Companies declared their willingness to finish the line to Fradley (p120).

The Oxford Canal was equally slow in being built, and problems developed over its junction with the Coventry. This was finally set at Longford, which meant that the two canals ran parallel for over a mile, each taking additional tolls for the goods carried. A more logical junction at Hawkesbury was eventually made in the 1830s.

The most important feature of the Coventry Canal was the fact that it passed through the Warwickshire coalfield. The northern end of the Oxford Canal also tapped this coalfield, though most of the coal to be carried south came from the Coventry Canal. When the Grand Junction was completed in 1805, the winding Oxford Canal compared badly with the newer wide navigation. Very large cargoes of coal were moving into the London area and improvements were certainly needed. These were at last put in hand in the 1830s. The northern section of the Oxford Canal was shortened by over 13 miles by cutting off the wide loops and building a new wide tunnel at Newbold, with towpaths on both sides. At Hillmorton there are the only three locks on this section of the line; these were duplicated to hasten the traffic.

The route

Starting from Fazeley, the Coventry Canal runs parallel to the A5 and climbs through two locks at Glascote. Disused collieries come into view at Polesworth and the navigation climbs through eleven locks at Atherstone to the longest level stretch in the country. Halfway up the locks, an arm runs out towards some railway sidings; some of the last coal to be carried in the Midlands was loaded here. I recall meeting Mr and Mrs Collins with a loaded pair of Blue Line boats having a terrible struggle to get along the silted-up canal. As they passed us, they said it had taken them 3 hours to come just over 2 miles. The attractive Hartshill workshops are shown on p141 and as Nuneaton is approached coal tips are replaced by stone from the Hartshill-quartzite quarries.

Beyond Nuneaton, the little Griff Arm comes in from the right. This is one of the many small canals and arms which tapped coal mines to the west of the main canal. All were built in the eighteenth century and none is now navigable. The Ashby Canal comes in from the east at Marston junction, bringing yet more coal, and the short Bedworth colliery arm comes in from the other side.

Hawkesbury is one of the most interesting junctions on the canal system. The Coventry and Oxford Canals are running parallel at this point and the boater must make a horseshoe turn of 180°. There is a fine cast-iron bridge carrying the towpath across the centre of the horseshoe and a well-known boatmen's inn at the side. A large, brick engine house formerly contained a Newcomen engine which was used for pumping water from the mines into the canal. This engine is now at Dartmouth in Devon, Newcomen's birthplace.

The first time we cruised through Hawkesbury was on a bank holiday in 1962, when all the boat people were taking a weekend off duty. Pairs of boats lined both sides of both canals and there was just room to cruise down the middle under watchful eyes. As I write this, a national rally of boats is planned to be held at Hawkesbury; there will then doubt-less be a similarly narrow channel but the pleasure boater will not be under such professional scrutiny. The Coventry Canal continues for 5 miles into Coventry where there is a fine basin and warehouses.

The most obvious features of the Oxford Canal are the numerous branches which wind off on both sides to return a little later. These are lengths of the original contour canal and graceful cast-iron bridges carry the towpath across each branch. The waterway misses the centre of Rugby, though it passes close to the town, and crosses the Stratford Avon on a high aqueduct. British Waterways offices and workshops stand beside the Hillmorton locks and the canal continues on a level to Braunston to join up with the Grand Union Canal.

These two canals, forming the easier part of the 'Bottom Road', are important to the pleasure boater as a through-route from north to south, although we prefer the much tougher BCN and Grand Union or the longer Leicester line. The main railway line from London to Crewe and beyond follows the Coventry and Oxford Canals. In the mighty days of steam we noted famous engines hurrying past us, drawing trains to north-west England, Scotland and to Holyhead. With the demise of the horse-drawn narrowboat and of the steam locomotive, we have lost so much of the attractions of bygone days.

(*opposite top*) Below Boulters lock on the Thames. The boats are waiting their turn to lock through; (*bottom*) the Hartshill maintenance depot on the Coventry Canal. The eighteenth-century buildings are contemporary with the canal

9

CRUISING RIVERS

The English canal system was built to bring goods by water to towns which were too far from navigable rivers. It extended the river-navigation system and in so doing crossed watersheds, joining one navigation to another. The first major canal in England connected the navigable waters of the Trent with the Mersey estuary, and later canals linked the Kennet with the Bristol Avon and the Thames with the Severn. In this way, the canal network links up with navigable rivers throughout the country and all those who plan a cruising holiday can include a river section.

Problems and considerations
There are a number of differences between rivers and canals which must be taken into consideration. Most rivers are deeper than most English canals and some are very much deeper. Thus children and non-swimmers should always wear some form of lifejacket and everyone should be prepared for the possibility of falling in. I swim regularly in the Thames and it was consequently a great joke when I fell in above a lock with all my clothes on, including wind-jammer and hat. The lock-keeper was concerned until he saw that I should come to no harm, but had I been a non-

(*opposite top*) The Compleat Angler, Marlow. The suspension bridge is on the right and *Rose of Sharon* is moored on the left; (*centre*) Newbold tunnel on the Oxford Canal. This wide tunnel with towpaths on both sides is on one of the straight cuts of 1829; (*bottom*) the Inglesham round-house at the junction of the Thames and the Thames & Severn Canal, *c*1917 (*Ware Collection, National Waterways Museum*)

swimmer the situation might have been different. A lifebelt on a long rope should be kept in a handy place so that help can be given to anyone if necessary.

Rivers flow while canals, with very few exceptions, do not. It therefore takes longer to cruise upstream than down and this should be taken into account when planning a trip. Furthermore, the flow can vary and at times it can be very strong indeed. On one warm summer's day we cruised out of the Avon into the Severn at Tewkesbury and set off upstream to Worcester with plenty of time in hand. We moored for lunch at Upton and I had a swim. I noticed that the flow was much faster than I had expected but, being a strong swimmer, thought little of it. The weather was settled and had been so for the previous day, but we learned later that there had been torrential rain in mid-Wales two days earlier and that much of this had run off into the upper reaches of the Severn. We set off upriver and were soon punching a very strong current. Large logs began to appear in mid-stream and we had to keep crossing the river to avoid the swiftest flow. We were never in danger and we carried a suitable anchor – an absolute necessity on all rivers – but our speed was eventually reduced to less than 1mph. We could have given up the struggle in the lock cut below Worcester but we pushed on to the canal locks and were quickly brought through by the observant lock-keeper. He told us that the river had risen 3½ft in as many hours. Our original plan had been to moor at the private landing stage by the Diglis Hotel but this was now far below the turbulent waters and we were thankful for the peace of the canal basin. It is much safer going upstream on a flooded river for the boater has more control of the boat. We had a similar experience on the Avon but moored safely above a lock to rings on vertical poles until the floods abated.

Rising waters and a swift current can also make the shooting of bridges unsafe. There is one notorious bridge on the River Nene at Higham Ferrers, though recently demolished, it is situated on a sharp curve so that the whole river flows through one narrow arch with sloping sides. Even when the river is low, the current quickens through the bridge and eddies occur. A national boat rally was held at Northampton in August 1971 and a number of boats, including our own *Rose of Sharon*, took the opportunity to explore the river. Once again heavy rain had fallen in the catchment area and the river had risen. As we came upstream towards Higham Ferrers bridge, people signalled to us to draw in to the side where we discovered that two powerful boats had tried to push through, only to be flung against the side. Several of us waited together for 24 hours, by which time the river authority had run off sufficient water to make the passage less hazardous.

Serious floods rarely happen in the summer but they do occur and rivers can overflow their banks. We have seen the Avon at Stratford extending for hundreds of yards across the water meadows. Boats should leave any river before this happens, since it is not impossible to cruise out of the main channel and be left high and dry on a field as the water recedes! Floods of this size rarely occur without warning.

We have mentioned rivers rising, but they can also fall. This has happened to us on both the Thames and the Nene whilst moored up to the bank for the night. On such occasions, we have been awakened by the sound of something falling over to find that the boat was tilting. I have had to put on my wellies, leap out onto the bank, loosen ropes and push off into deeper water. Such mishaps can also happen on a canal if you moor in a short pound above a lock with leaky gates or in one where the last boat has left the paddles up. Boaters have sometimes found themselves tilted at an alarming angle in a waterless channel.

Most rivers have weirs which are usually well marked, but they can be dangerous at flood time. The Thames weirs are well controlled and most of the lock cuts ensure that the boats are kept away from them. Those on the Trent and

Severn, though clearly marked, are much more open and a boat with a stalled engine can easily be swept onto them. Thrumpton weir on the Trent, a little below its confluence with the Soar, has claimed its victims and Cromwell weir below Newark has also proved difficult when the river is in flood. Both have recently been protected by a floating barrier. Every boat should carry an anchor, preferably attached to a chain, which should be available for immediate action *before* things get out of hand. The weight and type of anchor, and the length of chain or rope, depends upon the craft and the river to be cruised; advice can always be obtained from boatyards.

Boats have occasionally been known to shoot a flooding weir and be carried downstream to safety, though they are more often swung sideways and overturned. If the river is low, the edge of the weir is only inches below the surface and the boat will fetch up against it and be easily pulled off. When the water is deeper, however, the boat may run onto the weir-edge amidships, with the bow standing out over the water. Rescue is then very difficult and a boat with a very powerful engine is needed to pull the unfortunate craft off backwards. To repeat: a suitable anchor, dropped in time, will avoid all these problems.

Llanthony weir on the Severn at Gloucester can be a cause for alarm. Fortunately it is several hundred yards below the locked entrance into the docks, but the current can be very swift. Boats coming downstream and making for the Gloucester & Sharpness Canal can moor against the high wall on the left while they wait for the lock gates to open. In a fast-flowing current this is often easier said than done; the main object is to get a stern rope round the rungs of one of the ladders. A friend of ours with a full-length narrowboat secured a bow rope to a rung and the stern was swept right across the river. The lock-keeper is always on the lookout for boats, especially if the owner has had the foresight to phone beforehand and given some idea of his time of arrival.

The weirs mentioned above are across the whole width of the river except for the lock cut. On many rivers there are also side weirs where the water slips over one side of the channel. Examples are to be found on the Soar at Leicester, the Avon at Tewkesbury, the Nene, the Great Ouse and a number of other rivers. There is no danger attached to them in normal circumstances, but when the river is in flood, there is a strong pull sideways and the boat may be dragged against the weir. It may then be difficult to get back into the channel.

Another problem is the danger of running aground in shallows. Shallows are particularly common at points where tributaries enter the main river; such areas are called scours. There is one such scour on the Nene above Wellingborough which needs frequent dredging; on one occasion when we ran aground, I slipped in with a spade and dug my way through! On our many attempts to reach the summits of navigation of such rivers as the Thames, the Severn and the Great Ouse, we have had difficulties with sand and gravel banks and strong currents.

On all rivers it is necessary to recognise and understand the navigation markers which show the channel and shallows. On mooring, particularly when there is any notable current, the boat should always turn to meet the current where possible.

All these river features – the weirs, the currents, the deep water, the floods and the shallows – may deter the pleasure cruiser, but it would be a great pity if this were the case. Provided that the proper precautions are taken our navigable rivers are very safe. We love the extra depth where the boat glides along so easily, the extra width where boats may turn back, perhaps to slip into some backwater, and the ease with which we can be passed by a boater in more hurry than we are. Although some rivers are heavily polluted, many are clean enough for the swimmer who is careful to keep his head (and mouth) above water.

All the foregoing concerns the non-tidal rivers. Those that

are tidal – the Trent below Cromwell, the Thames below Teddington, the Great Ouse below Denver and others – have their own special problems. We have cruised from the Grand Union at Brentford to Teddington, and from Salter's Lode to Denver. With proper advice, and at suitable times, canal boats similar to ours cross the Wash, continue down the Thames to the Medway, and cruise the tidal Severn and Avon to Bristol. However, such journeys are beyond the scope of this book.

The Thames
The Thames is the most popular cruising river in the country and is normally entered from the canal system either at Oxford or at Brentford. For those anxious to cruise through London, it can also be reached from Regent's Dock at the east end of the Regent's Canal or from the River Lee. Navigation above Teddington is controlled by the Thames Water Authority and a separate licence must be taken out in advance. As London's water supply is largely dependent upon the Thames, there are stringent anti-pollution regulations and no waste waters or bilge pumpings are allowed to contaminate it under penalty of heavy fines.

History
The river has a long history of navigation. From Roman times it was a highway from London to the west, and in the Middle Ages flash locks were built in weirs to enable craft to reach Oxford and eventually Cricklade. In 1624, three pound locks were built between Abingdon and Oxford and the remains of one of these is still visible in Swift Ditch, a now disused channel at Abingdon. Several more pound locks were built between Maidenhead and Reading in the late eighteenth century; at the end of the century a number were built downstream as were some on the upper river below Lechlade. Finally, between 1811 and 1830, some more were constructed between Teddington and Cookham though

there were still flash locks in use.

My *Oarsman's and Angler's Map of the River Thames* of 1884 records five such flash locks above Oxford, each with a fall varying from 1 to 3ft. The sites of several more are marked. The wooden footbridges which are such a feature of the river were built alongside these sites.

The route

The Thames is navigable from the tideway to Lechlade and, with difficulty, a few miles beyond. At one time the navigation extended as far as Cricklade but this section ceased to be maintained when the Thames & Severn Canal opened in 1789. As I write this, there are moves to rebuild this attractive length of the navigation.

The entry from the Oxford Canal is by one of two routes. A short branch drops down through Isis lock and runs south to join one of the several channels into which the river divides in Oxford. This branch is crossed by a low-level railway line and boaters used to have to contact the railway officials to have the bridge swung. The line is little used today and the bridge is not normally across the navigation. The other entry is by the short length known as Duke's Cut below Duke's lock, a few miles west of the city centre. This runs through a stoplock to join another Thames backwater above King's lock. In the last century, the barges would bypass Duke's Meadow with its flash locks by using the Duke's Cut and Isis lock.

Entry to the Thames from the Grand Union Canal is through the large Brentford basin, which has warehouses along the east side and the towpath opposite. The locks are at the southern end and the lock-keeper will advise the best time to enter the river. A short channel below the locks leads to a further lock into the River Brent but this cannot be used at low tide. On our first trip into the tidal waters we wondered how much the current would affect us. In fact, there seemed to be so little that we had to watch the driftwood near the bank to be assured that there was any movement at all. Ours is a slow boat and the lock-keeper had advised us to go up to Teddington with the tide for it would take us much longer to punch both tide and stream. When water is low at Richmond bridge, it is necessary to pass through a lock on the east side but there was sufficient water on our trip for us to run straight through.

Teddington now marks both the limit of the tide and of the jurisdiction of the Port of London Authority; here the lock-keeper checks to see if the boater holds a Thames licence. He may also check to make sure that the craft conforms to the strict conditions imposed to avoid pollution. The Thames locks are all manned and it is as well to plan the trip to fit in with the hours of duty. Most locks are now operated by remote control though it is still possible and permissible to operate some manually after hours.

The 125 miles of navigable river from here to Lechlade divides for us into three sections. The lowest, from Teddington to Maidenhead, is beautiful but busy, with mooring problems and many large pleasure craft. We spent one night on a concrete mooring at Hampton Court and were thrown about so much by passing boats that we stayed ashore until things quietened down. Apart from the palace and its beautiful parkland, which has sloping stone walls making mooring impossible, the banks are heavily built up along this section and reservoirs line the river above it.

Staines used to be the upper limit of the City of London's jurisdiction and the river was lock-free and even within reach of high spring tides until the early nineteenth century. Perhaps the most historic section lies west of Staines, where the river flows round Magna Carta island at Runnymede and divides Windsor from Eton a few miles further up. The splendid Norman castle dominates the scene to the south and the tall Eton College chapel stands boldly to the north.

We always feel that Maidenhead and Boulter's lock mark the limit of the lower river, for the next section as far as

Oxford, although still busy and even more beautiful, is less crowded and superb moorings are much easier to find. The wooded reaches of Cliveden and Marlow, the straight mile below Henley, famous for the regatta, and woodlands again at Marsh lock, are of especial beauty. Throughout this section there are several riverside hotels and inns of the highest quality and it would be invidious to name any for fear of leaving others out. We had been warned that many of these hotels were a bit 'snooty'. We were cruising through Marlow at lunchtime and noted that the town mooring was fully occupied. On the opposite side we saw a large, expensive, sea-going cruiser on the private mooring of the Compleat Angler. We moored *Rose of Sharon* behind this craft and, wearing our boat clothes (clean but not yachts-men's flannels), made for the front entrance, wondering if we should be directed to the back! Instead, we received a warm and pleasant welcome and ate one of the best lunches that I ever remember tasting.

Reading is a very large town, sitting astride the river and it is one of the few places where industry encroaches. The Kennet enters beneath a railway bridge from the south-west. The river is as beautiful above Reading and narrows between Goring and Streatley to flow through a gap in the chalk hills. There is a wooden bridge between the two villages, the last of many similar bridges on the river, all now replaced by brick, stone or metal.

The Sinodon Hills are the farthest outliers of the Chilterns and Berkshire Downs and are surmounted by clumps of trees and an Iron Age hill fort. Dorchester, with its magnificent abbey church, lies on the north bank between the river and the Thame. The village is in a strategic position and dates back to Roman times. The backwaters of Clifton and Culham locks are famous for their remote beauty, though now the 'no mooring' signs are more common. The abandoned Wilts & Berks Canal enters beneath an iron bridge at Abingdon, a most attractive town.

The river changes once more at the ancient city of Oxford, which sadly turns its worst face to the navigable stream. The relatively low bridge at Osney keeps some of the larger craft from the upper reaches, though many hirers have now gone in for an unattractive craft which looks like a single-decker bus. With the steerer and his wheel enclosed at the front they are undoubtedly comfortable, though they often go too fast and take up excessive room in locks.

The river above Oxford is quite different from the lengths below. The stream itself is smaller and narrower and its flood plain is so wide that most of the villages were built on rising ground some distance from the river. Newbridge, near Standlake, is medieval and has two inns, one on each side of the river. Radcot bridge has arches so narrow that great care is necessary when the river is in flood. A boat coming down has right of way, since it is much easier for the one below to stop and give way.

Lechlade is close to the limit of navigation. Here the churchyard and gardens come right down to the north bank of the river, which is crossed at Halfpenny bridge where tolls for the road users were once demanded. There is an open area of grassland above the bridge along the south bank and cars can be parked well back from the river for picnic parties to enjoy the scene. The river is navigable for a further mile up to Inglesham to the junction with the derelict Thames & Severn Canal, now being gradually restored.

On two occasions we have attempted to push as far up as possible, even though the flash locks which gave sufficient depth of water to Cricklade were removed over a century ago. The *Oarsman's and Angler's Map of the River Thames* of 1884 notes that 'it is now possible in a fair season for pleasure boats to reach Cricklade or even beyond with comparatively little trouble'. On our first venture, in 1972, during a fine and dry spell, we cruised through a sharply winding river with high banks ablaze with flowers. Pearl was in the bows with a shaft to gauge the depth when we ran aground about a mile below Hannington bridge. There was just room to slip back and turn and we gave up the attempt.

Our next attempt was in 1977 when we reached Lechlade after a fairly wet spell. I note from my log that there was plenty of water with a quickening stream above Inglesham. With Kempsford church in sight the current increased, particularly on the bends, and we soon passed our former limit. The water shallowed and the current quickened still further when we ran aground on the site of a weir and our bows swung into the bank. No amount of pulling with ropes from either bank (I waded across the river) freed us so I took my spade to dig away the obstruction amidships. Pearl was concerned that I should not be able to climb on board again as the current freed us and carried the boat down river, but all was well and we slipped back until the stream was wide enough for us to turn. We now know that if those beautiful higher reaches are to be made navigable once more, locks will need to be constructed to slow the current and give proper depth.

The Wey

The River Wey was made navigable to Guildford in 1651 and to Godalming, 4 miles further upstream, in 1760. The entire navigation is now owned and maintained by the National Trust. It presents a very different aspect to the overcrowded lower Thames, for the locks – though still barge-sized – are much smaller and the whole channel is both narrower and shallower.

The Wey enters the Thames at Weybridge below Shepperton lock and the navigation channel is narrow and half-hidden by trees. It turns sharply to the right where there is a short mooring from which the steerer may walk up to the lock-house to pay his toll. A further sharp turn to the left brings the boat into a deep lock with very fierce paddles. The entrance channel itself may not be deep enough for some boats and its level can be raised by closing gates below the mooring and bringing down more water from above.

Much of the first 6 miles above Thames lock consists of an artificial cut which the river enters and leaves at a few points only. Halfway along this section, the Basingstoke Canal comes in from the west; this beautiful waterway is now being fully restored to navigation and should be open once more in a few years' time.

There is a flood lock at Walsham and the gates are left open at both ends in normal conditions. From this point south-wards the navigation follows the river closely except for the short lock cuts. The river itself is deeper and clearer than the artificial cuts and is more suitable for mooring. There are villages within reach and attractive riverside pubs. The major town is Guildford, which is blessed with excellent moorings; it sits astride the river and all the shops are within a few minutes' walk. A gin has been preserved on the old quay, a treadmill which once worked a waterside crane. We were amused at the contrast between the heavy traffic in the town and the quiet river.

The loveliest part of the river is above Guildford, and we found a little island and backwater beside St Catherine's lock which made a perfect mooring. The entrance to the Wey & Arun Canal, long since abandoned but now being restored, is a mile further south. There is a good mooring on the northern edge of Godalming and, though this is the terminus of the navigation beyond which one must not cruise, the wide, deep river above looks navigable. The 20 miles of river from the Thames to Godalming with its 16 locks is ideal for an unhurried week's holiday. When we last cruised it in 1977, we allowed ten days and found that it was worth every minute.

The Kennet

This river joins the Thames at Reading; it was made navigable to Newbury in 1715 and later became part of the Kennet & Avon Canal. Restoration of the whole waterway to Bath is being carried out successfully and a number of lengths are already fully navigable. At the time of writing the Kennet is navigable for about 12 miles and is worth a quick visit, but cruising will be really worthwhile when it is reopened to Newbury and beyond.

Blake's lock, the first to be reached, belongs to the Thames Water Authority and is normally manned but the rest are owned by the British Waterways Board. The river runs through the heart of Reading and there are short moorings for shopping. For some miles beyond the town the river is never far from the M4 motorway, but when it finally turns away it runs through attractive rural scenery. Several of the locks are the original turf-sided structures, though we were told that these would eventually be replaced. There are a number of very heavy swing bridges which must first be closed to traffic and then raised slightly with jacks before they can be swung. We found that the water was particularly clear and clean and, in places, fast-flowing. The cruise back downriver was much faster than the cruise up.

The Rivers Lee and Stort

The Lee reaches the tidal waters of the Thames at Limehouse but can be entered from the Regent's and Hertford Union Canals. When we cruised it in 1969 it was said to be the busiest commercial navigation in the country, with many tugs towing strings of barges; today there is much less traffic. The river itself is a very ancient navigation and was immensely important to London both as a carrier of corn and ale and as a provider of water. The first improvement Act was in 1424 and the first pound lock was built at Waltham Abbey in 1574. The New River was constructed in 1608 to carry drinking water from just above Ware to the city and now the lower reaches are lined with reservoirs. During the great plague of 1665, boatmen continued to carry corn to the city and for this Charles II granted them the freedom of the Thames. The most attractive stretch is the four miles from

Ware to Hertford, though the lower reaches are full of interest and much of the river is now bordered by the Lee Valley Country Park. When we were cruising, barges were pulled by tractors from the towpath and we had to choose an offside position, preferably above a lock, for mooring.

The Stort enters the Lee below Rye House Inn where once the Great Bed of Ware slept twelve people. Furthermore, it was from here that the unsuccessful Rye House Plot was hatched to kill Charles II and his brother James on their way back from the races at Newmarket. The Stort is a much more rural river than the Lee, its navigation dating from an Act of 1759. It has several very beautiful water mills and malt houses, mostly in backwaters by the locks, and it is easy to picture the countryside as London's larder. The terminus is at Bishop's Stortford which, unlike Hertford, turns its back on the navigation. When we were there there was no obvious way from the towpath to the town centre and, as it was raining, we quickly turned back to the lovely village of Sawbridgeworth.

We spent six days on the two rivers and found them well worth exploring. Several of the locks on the lower part of the Lee are automatic but those higher up and on the Stort have fairly heavy paddles. The Stort is liable to changes in level, and as certain bridges are fairly low it is worth checking in advance.

The Warwickshire Avon
History
The Avon is navigable for some 46 miles, from a few miles above Stratford to its junction with the River Severn at Tewkesbury. A Trust has been formed to get permission to extend the navigation to Warwick and to link up with the Grand Union Canal but, at the time of writing, no decisions have been made. The navigation itself has a long and chequered history. As early as 1636, William Sandys of Fladbury obtained permission to build the necessary locks

and water gates to enable small barges to reach Stratford. In 1760, George Perrott bought the navigation from Evesham to the Severn and thereafter two separate companies existed. The upper navigation deteriorated steadily and was in so bad a state in the 1870s that the owners, the Great Western Railway Company, refused to charge tolls. The locks collapsed and the weirs were breached, so that only craft that could be carried round the obstructions were able to use the river at all. The lower navigation remained clear of railway ownership and though it also deteriorated it was usable well into this century.

The subsequent history of these two sections of the river makes a very different story. The Lower Avon was bought by Mr Douglas Barwell in 1950 and the Lower Avon Navigation Trust was formed. Money was raised, locks were repaired or rebuilt, and the whole length to Evesham was reopened in 1962. The lock above Evesham bridge, ostensibly part of the Upper Avon, was rebuilt two years later.

After the reopening of the Stratford Canal by Her Majesty Queen Elizabeth the Queen Mother in 1964, the Upper Avon Navigation Trust was formed. The task of restoration was much more formidable, for new locks in different places were needed and the river had to be maintained at a lower level. The work was carried out by David Hutchings of Stratford Canal fame and the Upper Avon was reopened in 1974, once more by the Queen Mother. It is now possible to cruise the Avon from the canal network or from the Severn and return by a different route.

The route

The river at Tewkesbury splits into two branches: the easterly flows parallel to the main road and past a mill to enter the Severn below the town; the westerly branch enters the Severn above the town and it is from this branch that the entrance lock is constructed. Both above and below the lock are mooring lengths and it is a short walk across the little eighteenth-century iron bridge into the town.

The Avon is a wandering river, occupying a wide valley. The lower reaches are dominated by the 1,000ft-high Bredon Hill, but such are the meanderings of the river that the hill seems first to lie on one side and then the other, sometimes ahead and sometimes behind. The beautiful Eckington bridge, built in the Middle Ages, contrasts with the high, wide span which carries the M5 motorway across the valley. This is a region of orchards and of abbey buildings, from the splendid church at Tewkesbury and the half-standing church at Pershore to the isolated tower which dominates the scene at Evesham.

The Avon is a sailing river and at weekends the dinghies are all out tacking from side to side. It is also a fishing river and during the season the anglers line the banks. Rather sadly, the space for mooring is restricted and most owners of private land beside the river post 'no mooring' signs. Furthermore, the lovely towns of Pershore and Evesham, each with a wide river frontage, offer only the most restricted moorings which fill up very early. Suitable moorings have been made however in the lock cuts of the Upper Avon and Stratford itself has plenty of room.

Taken altogether the river is one of exceptional beauty and is at its best for the pleasure boater in the spring, when it is fairly quiet and coarse fishing is out of season.

The Severn
History
This river has been used as a water highway for many hundreds of years. The mighty tides of the lower reaches used to sweep up as far as Upton, and even Worcester. The smaller Severn sailing trows, towed at times by gangs of

(*opposite top*) Telford's cast-iron Holt Fleet bridge on the Severn; (*centre*) Fladbury lock and mill on the Lower Avon; (*bottom*) Newark town lock and castle on the Trent. The walls are high for mooring but are lower on the town wharf below the bridge

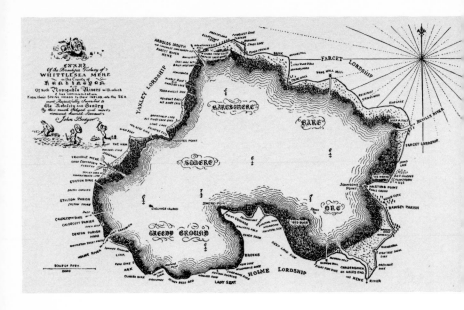

(above) Chart of the now-vanished Whittlesey Mere in 1786 where Lord Orford and his friends sailed in the Fens (*The Syndics of Cambridge University Library*); (below) Daneway portal of Sapperton tunnel on the Thames & Severn Canal where Bliss moored in the 1890s (*Ware Collection, National Waterways Museum*)

halers, could reach Shrewsbury and sometimes the pool of Welshpool in the eighteenth century. Horse towpaths were built between Shrewsbury and Gloucester between 1772 and 1812, as were locks between Gloucester and Stourport in the 1840s and 1850s. Though the opening of the Staffs & Worcs Canal took some of the trade from the upper river, Ironbridge continued to be a major transhipment port, where goods were transferred from the tub-boats of Coalbrookdale to the trows on the river. The tub-boat canals at Coalbrookdale were never linked with the Severn though they eventually joined the rest of the canal network by the opening of the Newport branch of the Shroppie; traffic above Stourport dwindled. It is now difficult to take a pleasure boat as far as Bewdley bridge without running firmly aground.

The route

The pleasure cruiser can enter the Severn from the Staffs & Worcs Canal at Stourport, from the Worcester & Birmingham Canal at Worcester and from the Avon at Tewkesbury. It will also be possible to cruise in from Droitwich when restoration of that canal is complete. At Gloucester, the Gloucester & Berkeley Canal cuts out the most difficult tidal stretch of the river and it may be possible one day to enter here from the Thames by way of the Thames & Severn and Stroudwater Canals. The river is strongly tidal below Sharpness and cruising these waters is beyond the scope of this book.

The Severn at Stourport looks so wide and deep to the boater used to canals. The narrow locks from the canal basin are used and the river is seen immediately to differ markedly from the Thames in the height of its banks. Though much has been done recently to control water levels, the river is still subject to considerable flooding. There is a floodmark dated 1947 on a wall by Worcester Cathedral which shows that the water can even overtop these banks. There are plenty of excellent places to tie up for the night along by the Worcester racecourse, and room at Upton both on the town mooring and in the marina. Tewkesbury has also been mentioned as a good, safe place and there are several riverside inns with their own moorings.

The locks are worked by remote control by lock-keepers who call down from dizzy heights to ask the name of the boat and the licence number. There are several high bridges; the two built of iron by Thomas Telford at Holt Fleet and Tewkesbury are described on p65. The banks are lined with huge limestone blocks in many places, brought from the Avon gorge by specially constructed square-sailed barges. One such barge, the *Harriett*, built of wood with a transom stern, lies on the banks of the Severn at Purton.

The river divides into two channels, the Partings, above Gloucester and the narrower, easterly one is followed to the city. The spring tides overtop this section and there may be quite a fast current in either direction. We enjoy a trip on the Severn, but use it most frequently as a through route from one canal to another or to the River Avon.

The Soar
Turning now to the East Midlands, the River Soar, which forms part of the Grand Union Canal network, is a waterway that we cruise regularly. The navigation from Leicester to the Trent is only 25 miles and nearly a third of this consists of artificial cuts but the actual river sections compare with the upper Thames and the Avon. The channel is clear and many of the low banks drop straight into deep water. Any river running through towns as large as Leicester and Lough-borough is bound to attract some rubbish and pollution but there is little evidence of this.

The river south of Leicester is a winding stream but as soon as it becomes a navigation below King's lock it broadens and deepens. Through the whole of Leicester, from Aylestone to Belgrave, the river keeps winding in and out of the navigation and there are several notices warning of side weirs. The channel is straight as it flows along by the Boulevard to West Bridge but sadly the city makes very little use of its river, which could be improved greatly. The river leaves the navigation above North lock to flow through the attractive Abbey Park, the central site of the 1967 national boat rally when 400 craft of all sizes congregated.

A lengthy artificial cut at Syston is used by barges and narrowboats for the carriage of gravel, and the River Wreak, once navigable to Melton Mowbray, comes in further north. Mountsorrel is famous for its granite quarries, and disused loading points can be seen below the lock. The river and the artificial cut divide again north of Barrow, the Soar sweeping round east of Loughborough and the navigation running through the town. The junction with the Leicester section and the older Loughborough navigation is T-shaped and boats often fail to turn the sharp corner and ram the wall opposite. Loughborough basin to the left is very central for shopping.

Normanton is the next village and from there northwards the river is at its most beautiful. It is worth spending a few days here gently cruising past green meadows, mooring up and calling at the inns whose gardens sweep down to the water. The slight fall at Redhill lock carries the river to the level of the Trent. Redhill is named after the low hill on its east bank where deep-red Keuper marl is seamed with veins of alabaster. The final junction is just above Thrumpton weir and boats must swing sharply to the left to reach the Trent navigation.

The Trent
History
Like the Thames and Severn, the Trent has been navigable for at least part of its course from earliest times. Wilden Ferry and Cavendish Bridge, where the A6 road from Derby to Leicester crosses the river, was long considered the upward limit of navigation. In 1699 two locks were built, one at

King's Mills and the other at Burton, to bring barges up to that town. When the eastern end of the Trent & Mersey Canal was completed in 1770 it created an alternative route to Burton and the upper section of the river fell into disuse. In the late eighteenth century the navigation below Cavendish Bridge was gradually improved by the addition of locks and a towpath, and between 1906 and 1926 larger locks were built below Nottingham.

The route
The Trent is similar to the Severn with its wide, deep channel and high banks. It is not a river to moor in but rather one to use as a link between the canals, the Soar and the Lincolnshire waterways. There are, however, sections of great beauty with high, tree-clad cliffs.

Boats from the Trent & Mersey Canal enter at a crossroads. The Trent is straight ahead, coming in round a sharp corner from the right. It is very wide at this point and the towpath passes over the upper section on a footbridge. The M1 motorway crosses at a great height above the water and the first of the lock cuts is entered through a flood lock. This is Sawley, which has a boatyard and a huge marina; two locks, side by side, carry the boats back into the river. There is a major navigation junction a mile below Sawley with Trent lock on the left leading into the Erewash Canal. Cranfleet cut, part of the Trent Navigation, is ahead on the left and Thrumpton Weir is to the right, with the turning off to the Soar just above the weir.

Four miles of winding river below Cranfleet leads to Beeston lock and weir, and from Beeston 6 miles of canal run through Nottingham itself. Knowing Leicester well, I had expected this to be rather a dismal navigation and was pleasantly surprised with what I found. The canal runs through the huge Boots (the chemists) estate and then turns to join the Nottingham Canal at Lenton Chain. The Nottingham Canal north of the junction was abandoned in 1937 and has now been filled in. Below Castle lock is a fine series of warehouses, one of which houses a canal museum; this places special emphasis on Fellows, Morton & Clayton as it was here that the carrying company had its Nottingham depot. After another half-mile, the canal takes a sharp turn to the right and drops down Meadow Lane lock into the river. Trent Bridge is on the right and parkland sweeps down to the water above the bridge. Nottingham makes much of its lovely river and it was here that a national boat rally was held in 1974. The abandoned Grantham Canal enters the Trent almost opposite Meadow Lane lock.

Running eastwards, the river is soon out in the country and before it reaches Holme locks, it passes the international rowing course of Holme Pierpont set in parklands. The lock cut makes a good mooring for this area. The huge locks in the river look so deep owing to their high walls and gates; they are very necessary, for this river in flood can rise many feet. Lock-keepers control the locks, which have fierce sluices, and the pleasure boat is advised to moor as far back as possible in them when coming up. There are, of course, no problems when dropping down. Once, when approaching one of the locks from below, I gave a toot on my horn to make my presence known. When nothing happened, Pearl suggested that I should give a really good blow and this I did. Seconds later came a shout from above, 'All right Gabriel, I heard you!'

The riverside villages with their attractive inns are not always easy to reach from the water, for either the banks are too high or the water is too shallow at the sides. The lock-keepers ask your destination and it is obvious that there are few moorings on this stretch. We were delighted to find Farndon Harbour in a disused gravel pit where we were allotted an excellent berth for a couple of nights.

The river divides at Newark and the narrower navigable section runs off to the right and passes right beneath the ruined walls of Newark castle. Moorings are either against high vertical walls or on the town wharf below the bridge.

Five miles below the Newark Nether lock – where the other branch of the river rejoins – is Cromwell lock and weir and the head of the tideway. We have not continued into tidal waters and boaters proposing to do this should get advice on the tides from the lock-keeper.

The Nene

The Fen rivers are almost cut off from the rest of the canal network; almost but not quite. A 5-mile branch of the Grand Union Canal drops down from Gayton junction through 17 narrow locks to join the Nene at Northampton. Each lock has a fall of only about 7ft and the first 12 are very close together. The canal then flows beneath the M1 motorway and it is singularly quiet beneath the huge arch. The last 5 locks are well spaced out and the junction is reached above Northampton bridge.

In its lower reaches, from Peterborough through Dog-in-a-Doublet lock and Wisbech to the Wash, the Nene is a true Fen river and is tidal below that lock. Above Peterborough, it is a delightful waterway winding through water meadows and past charming villages. It was in the eighteenth century that attempts were made to make the river navigable to Northampton, and by 1761 these were successful. Thirty-four locks and twelve staunches (flash locks) were constructed, but most were rebuilt in the 1830s. There is a good example of one of these locks at Wansford, and the remains of a staunch can be seen at Perio with 'T.A. 1836' carved into the stonework. The navigation deteriorated during the next hundred years, but in 1931 the newly established Nene Catchment Board replaced all the locks and staunches with the present locks which have mitred top gates and a guillotine gate at the bottom. More recently, the Anglian Water Authority has replaced each of the top three locks in Northampton with mitred gates top and bottom and has cut special drainage channels to control flooding.

Northampton is a large town and it makes the most of its beautiful river. The whole riverside is parkland, with excellent moorings within easy reach of the shops. Below the town the locks come thick and fast and it must be said that those with guillotine gates are hard work. They have to be left empty for drainage purposes, which means that the gate must be lowered and raised for each passage, whether up or down. Each action requires the big handle to be turned from anything between 80 to 150 turns and the upper mitred gates have had new paddles recently fitted which require 75 turns up and the same number down again. The pleasure boater should never be in a hurry or this would be a great imposition!

Once below Wellingborough, which also has attractive parkside moorings, the locks become more spaced out. With the ancient stone bridges, the riverside villages built of the warm-brown Northamptonshire ironstone and the fields and woods reaching down to the water, the river scenery is outstanding. Perhaps the reaches on either side of Lilford lock are the most beautiful of any in the country and the village of Wadenhoe with its waterside inn completes the scene.

Oundle is a splendid old town with a marina in a flooded gravel pit beside an attractive park. The river runs in a wide horseshoe bend for 3 miles before returning to the other side of the town. The great tower of Fotheringhay church dominates the next stretch and a small mound is all that is left of the castle where Richard III was born and Mary Queen of Scots resided before her execution. The name *Perio*, meaning 'I perish', is said to originate from the unhappy queen's exclamation when she first saw Fotheringhay castle.

The river flows beneath the high bridges of the A1 trunk road at the village of Wansford-in-England. Here the story is told of a man who fell asleep on a haycock which was washed downriver in floods. When he awoke and was told that he was in Wansford, he asked 'Wansford in England?' Needless to say, the splendid old hostelry here is called *The Haycock*.

The Nene flows past more charming villages and past the Nene Valley Railway to Peterborough which, like Northampton, makes the most of its river with a mile of parkland moorings. The last 5 miles to Dog-in-a-Doublet are straight and of little interest. For anyone proposing to cruise this beautiful river, plenty of time should be set aside. The locks have already been mentioned and, more important, there is a need to explore some of the loveliest villages in the country. The river deserves at least a fortnight, though one might easily spend a whole month on its waters.

The Great Ouse

The Great Ouse and its tributaries are truly Fen rivers for much of their courses. A great deal of Fen drainage work was carried out in the seventeenth century, much of which consisted of the straightening of the river courses. The Great Ouse below Denver Sluice is tidal and the long, straight Old and New Bedford rivers bring surplus waters from Earith, 20 miles away. The New Bedford river, though tidal, is itself navigable, though of little interest. The non-tidal Old West river takes a more winding course above Denver and finally locks up to rejoin the straight stretches at Earith. In recent years, since the terrible floods of 1947, Denver Sluice has been extended and a wide cut-off channel runs round the east side of the Fens to carry off surplus water. The whole structure is built to ensure that such flood damage should not occur again.

Pleasure craft can be hired on the Great Ouse and there are many miles of delightful cruising. For boaters visiting from the canal network, the route is down the Nene and the Middle Level (pp172–4). There is a lock at Salter's Lode, from Well Creek into the river, and a navigable sluice from the Old Bedford river. The latter can only be passed for a few minutes each day when the tidal Ouse makes a level, and though the period through the lock is also limited it is a little longer. The tidal river flows very fast at this point, the waters running out for approximately nine hours and coming in for about three. On our visit, we phoned the lock-keeper at Salter's Lode from Nordelph and were told when to arrive. We reached the lock a little early and were astonished to see that the river was still far below between mud banks. It seemed to be only a few minutes later when it had made a level and the lock-keeper raised the guillotine gate. A short, crooked channel took us into the swiftly flowing river and we reached Denver Sluice, three-quarters of a mile away, in no time. The lock has gates which open either way and we were soon locked through into still waters.

On our return journey, we checked the best time with the Denver lock-keeper and he phoned Salter's Lode to tell them to expect us. The Salter's Lode lock-keeper waved us to go some distance past the entrance channel and to turn and enter with the tide. Once in the channel, we needed full reverse to avoid bumping the side but the lock was open and we slid in. This all sounds rather frightening, but with helpful lock-keepers we entered and left the Ouse with very little trouble.

The river above Denver is level and lockfree for 36 miles. It is known as the Old West river and it flows between high banks set well back to provide an enlarged channel in time of flood. The city of Ely stands on its 'island', a patch of high ground which was truly an island before the Fens were drained. The magnificent cathedral stands on the hilltop and can be seen for miles; the ancient city is so small that it can be explored thoroughly. There are excellent moorings reserved for visiting boaters.

The junction with the Cam is 3 miles above Ely and one of the great beam engines, formerly used to drain the Fens, is a few miles further on at Stretham. It is housed in a fine engine house which is open to the public. The engine used to turn a scoop-wheel to lift water to the higher level.

Hermitage lock is at the end of the long level reach and the boat is *lifted* into a 2-mile stretch of river that is still tidal! It is connected directly to the New Bedford river; the tide reaches this point but with only a slight rise and fall. The river then climbs out of the Fens and the locks begin once more. The lower ones are operated by lock-keepers and some are power-operated. The riverside villages are very beautiful and each has excellent moorings. It is this part of the river that is most attractive for river cruising and plenty of time should be allowed.

The river divides into two at Bedford, making a long island of parkland with a lock through the centre. Bedford is a large town and we all found it too easy to lose our way shopping! We continued up the river as far as Kempston Mill but the water was getting shallower and the current increasing. We finally went aground and had to float down backwards to turn. It is not many miles as the crow flies to the Grand Union Canal and it would not be difficult to make the river navigable to Wolverton where some form of lift could effect a junction.

For those planning a cruising holiday, a week or a fortnight's trip will enable the boater to visit many of the most attractive parts of the river. Coming from the canals demands a fairly long holiday: we awaited my retirement and then took three months.

The Cam and the Lodes

The Cam forks off to the south-east from the Great Ouse at Popes Corner and is a typical Fen river for the first few miles. There are three locks on the navigation: the first, at Bottisham, belongs to the Anglian Water Authority and the other two to the University, who make a special charge. Between the two University locks (Baits Bite and Jesus) there are many oarsmen and oarswomen but there is plenty of room if the steerer is alert. Hire boats are not allowed above Jesus lock though the navigation extends to Magdalene Bridge. Private boats are permitted, but there were so many punts that we moored and walked in from there.

Several navigable lodes run into the lower reaches of the

170

Cam from the east and these are believed to have been dug in Roman times. Each extends to a village just outside the limits of the Fens. The three most navigable are entered through Reach lock, modern and electrically operated. We cruised to the termini of both Reach and Burwell lodes and explored the attractive villages but it is Wicken that is really worth visiting. Wicken lode runs through Wicken Fen, which is owned and maintained by the National Trust. It is an area of Fenland that has been kept in its natural state, and it is a perfect haven for bird, insect and plant life. Here you can appreciate how the Fens must have looked before they were drained. Reeds for thatching are harvested and for the first time we heard snipe drumming; we even hoped to hear the bittern boom but were disappointed. We were there in early June and were told that this is a good time to come, for the mosquitoes become troublesome later.

The Ouse tributaries
The Rivers Lark, Little Ouse and Wissey were once all navigable further upstream than they are today. The Fenland sections are all that is left now, for the locks and staunches of the upper lengths have fallen into disuse. The Lark has a single electric lock at Isleham and it is possible to cruise up as far as Judes Ferry, where there is a delightful inn with river moorings. I walked on up the river for a mile to Kings Staunch to examine the remains of one of the best preserved of the nineteenth-century staunches. The lock-house has the initials 'T.G.C. 1842' carved into the portal and it is now privately occupied. The initials refer to Sir Thomas Cullum who owned and improved the navigation to Bury St Edmunds. The present owners of the house kindly allowed me to take photographs.

The Little Ouse, or Brandon river, was once navigable to Thetford and there is a now-unnavigable lode to Lakenheath. The river passes through wild, open country; its high banks are well back and miniature lakes lie between them and the channel. We were amused at the many swans which all took flight when we approached them. Before reaching the terminus – an impassable sluice and weir a mile short of Brandon – we crossed over the cut-off channel on an aqueduct. We had to cruise beneath a sluice which would be lowered in time of flood so that the river could be diverted into this channel.

The Wissey is the smallest of these tributaries. A mile from its junction is Hilgay, a charming village on a hill which was also a Fen island once. The river banks are covered with comfrey of all different shades of colour and we were lucky to see them in full bloom. The channel runs through two lakes or broads and is dominated by the towering Wissington sugar-beet factory, which used to have its beet delivered by barge. The navigation terminates now at Stoke Ferry, which seemed a rather unattractive village, though boats were moored a mile further up at the more attractive Whittington. Once more we had to cross the cut-off channel, passing beneath the guillotine gate.

The Middle Level
The Middle Level navigations are an intricate series of Fenland drains, most of which were cut in the seventeenth century and enlarged later. They also contain lengths of the old courses of the Rivers Nene and Ouse as they wander through the Fens. To cope with floods they are nearly all high-banked and many miles are below sea-level. At first they sound uninteresting, but they have great charm of their own, some of it associated with the banks themselves, which are ablaze with flowers throughout most of the summer, and some of it owing to the wide and beautiful skies unhidden by hills or trees. They also have great historical interest which becomes apparent when one appreciates the purpose for which they were cut.

The drains provide through routes between the two rivers, Nene and Ouse, though boaters with time to spare should go exploring. The entrance from the Nene is through Stan-ground Sluice, a lock where the length restricts entry to boats whose maximum length is 49ft. You lock down into the drains and the lock-keeper should be notified about 48 hours before arrival to ensure that there is sufficient depth of water.

The first town is Whittlesey, a few miles beyond the lock, and we found this to be a charming place with excellent moorings beyond the notorious bend. This is a sharp turn in a much-narrowed channel and we were warned that we should have difficulty getting round. Actually we were round it before we had realised that we had reached it! Ashline lock drops the level even lower and we were then below sea-level in the main drainage system of the Fens. From here there are several routes, the most direct through the so-called Twenty Foot drain, now much wider, to Upwell, Outwell and Well Creek. The more attractive is through Flood's Ferry to the old course of the Nene and through March to Upwell, for the river winds and the drain is straight. March is another attractive town, the home of the Middle Level Watermen's Club, who welcomed us to their moorings.

Marmont Priory lock, north of March, lifts the boat out of the deepest Fens and to the two villages of Upwell and Outwell which have a very Dutch appearance. Well Creek continues, and crosses the main drain on an aqueduct to lead on to the tiny village of Nordelph, which has excellent moorings opposite the inn and beside the village shop. We were interested to see that this opened at 6am for the benefit of the farming community.

The Middle Level Watermen speak fondly of their cruising waters which extend for over 100 miles, and they are certainly quiet and remote. They are at their best for the boater out of the coarse-fishing season (15 March–15 June) for they are much loved by anglers, particularly at weekends.

The name Middle Level often arouses curiosity. In the mid-seventeenth century, the fourth and fifth Earls of

Bedford (the latter became the first duke) divided the vast area of the Fenland into the North Level, which extended from the River Glen to Morton's Leam (a cut parallel to the present tidal section of the River Nene); the Middle Level from there to the Old Bedford river; and the South Level east and south of the Old Bedford river. It is through the Middle Level that so many of the drains are open to navigation.

The Weaver
The little Cheshire river has been an important commercial navigation for more than two centuries. Flowing through the salt towns of Winsford and Northwich, it was made navigable by Act of Parliament in 1721 and eleven weirs with locks were built. There were improvements during both the eighteenth and nineteenth centuries. In the 1870s the whole navigation was deepened and the original locks replaced by four pairs of locks built large enough for much bigger craft. Traces of many of the earlier locks can still be seen, notably beneath Acton Bridge and at Pickerings; here gate recesses are visible at the side and the little pigeon-hole ladders mark where boaters could climb out of the lock. The Anderton Boat Lift was built at this period to link with the Trent & Mersey Canal.

The usual entry to the river is down the boat lift, though at the time of writing this is out of action owing to repairs. Until 1965 it was possible to lock down from the Bridge-water Canal at Runcorn but the locks have now been closed and filled in. The only other entrance is from the Manchester Ship Canal through Weston Point docks or Weston Marsh lock.

Anderton is a small but important inland port, with wharves beside the boat lift and the quays of the ICI Winnington and Wallerscote works opposite. The lift is fully described on p58. Ships of around 1,000 tons have recently reached Anderton from various countries overseas.

Pleasure boats can cruise upstream from Anderton to

Northwich, which has good shopping moorings, and on through Hartford to Winsford. The upper part of the river is lined with abandoned saltworks and it is easy to imagine the old salt steam packets and their barges carrying away the salt. The ICI salt mine is on the west bank below Winsford bridge, and above the bridge is a wide area of subsidence occupied by the Winsford flashes. The bottom flash is a large lake used by a sailing club and this is as far as the pleasure cruiser can go.

The run down the river is both beautiful and interesting. There are the big locks of Saltersford and Dutton and the wide, deep river flows through rural scenery. Often there is not a house or even a farm building in sight. A cut through to Frodsham terminates in an abandoned lock which makes a quiet mooring off the main stream. There is Sutton Level lock, no longer used, and now the final resting place for many interesting old wooden craft. The final stretch passes another huge ICI works and continues on to the Weston Point docks, passing Weston Marsh lock on the way. The fact that large cargo boats may be met on the river below Anderton need not deter the pleasure cruiser for there is plenty of room for both. It is important, however, to moor for the night either above Anderton or off the main channel.

There are other rivers which may be explored from the canal system. We have not taken *Rose of Sharon* up the Yorkshire Ouse or the Derwent or the Fen Rivers Witham and Welland, and the tidal waters need not prove an obstacle. The Medway can be reached from the Thames estuary, though a pilot or considerable personal experience, together with a suitable craft, is needed. Many of these rivers are within the reach of towed craft and there are suitable launching slipways but such trips are beyond the scope of this book.

It is certainly hoped that the pleasure boater who loves canal cruising will find equal pleasure in exploring our river navigations.

10

PLEASURE CRUISING IN BYGONE DAYS

Boating for pleasure has a very long history. We know, for instance, that in the year 922 King Edgar steered his own barge from his castle at Chester on the River Dee to St John's church, rowed by eight vassal kings and that the whole river was thronged with boats. Royal barges have a long history and in Tudor times, King Henry VIII was frequently rowed upriver from London to Hampton Court.

Samuel Pepys's diaries are full of notes about the use of the Thames, both for communication and for pleasure purposes. He wrote, for instance, on 14 September 1661: 'Before we had dined, comes Sir R. Slingsby and his lady and a great deal of company to take my wife and I out by barge to show them the King's and the Duke's yachts. We had great pleasure seeing all four yachts, viz. those two and two dutch ones.' On 30 May 1662, he wrote: 'I took my wife and Sarah and Will by water with some vituals as low as Gravesend.' A rather different comment occurs on 14 September that year: 'By water to Whitehall, by the way hearing that the Bishop of London had given a very strict order against boats going on Sundays and, as I came back again, we were examined by the masters of the company in another boat, but I told them who I was [Secretary to the Admiralty].'

An eighteenth-century cruise
One of the most charming descriptions of an early pleasure cruise occurs in *Lord Orford's Voyage round the Fens* in 1774, published in 1868 by A. W. Childers. The book is actually

three separate journals, one by His Lordship, and the others by two of his guests. Lord Orford lived at Lakenheath and the cruise was started from Lakenheath Lode which links with the Little Ouse or Brandon river. The fleet was a large one, consisting of the sailing craft *The Whale, The Alligator, The Shark* and *The Dolphin* together with the horse-boat and victualler *The Cocoa Nut*, three tenders *Pristus, Centaurus* and *Chimera* and a bumketch named *Fireaway*. They had a single Fen horse for towing named Hippopotamus!

They set off on Sunday 17 July soon after midday, being towed by the horse down the lode and entered the Little Ouse an hour later. They cruised a little way down the river and moored to fish. Weighing anchor at three, they continued on down to the Great Ouse and dropped anchor again at 4.30 to dine. They 'passed through Denver Sluice without accident' – the sluice had a navigation lock at that time but it must have taken some time to bring the whole fleet through – and finally arrived at Salter's Lode at 9.30. They hoped to anchor in the lode but were prevented 'by the low water and the gangs of barges which interrupted our passage'. Salter's Lode was then a sluice without a lock and could only be negotiated when the tide was level with the waters inside.

They brought the whole fleet through Salter's Lode successfully about five next morning and carried on along what is now known as Well Creek, then one of the branches of the River Nene. They continued through Outwell and Upwell and through to March where they anchored for dinner. March was described as the handsomest town they had seen and this description still holds today, though the river flows through it between high banks.

Four miles beyond March, after anchoring for the night, they turned into Whittlesey Dyke, a Fen drain, but then returned to follow the old River Nene again towards Benwick described as 'prettily situated on each side of the river, the grounds having a fertile appearance'. In several places they met bridges too low for the fleet to pass and in each case they raised the bridge 'with jacks and proper engines' and repaired it again when they had passed through. Their craft were probably a great deal higher than the Fen lighters, even if they could lower their masts, and it would seem that such pleasure craft were not very common.

The next day they reached Whittlesey Mere which was described by His Lordship as being 4 miles long, 2 to 3 miles wide and with a winding coastline of up to 24 miles. They had sailing races and anchored for fishing, for it was said that the Mere was full of fish; this was undoubtedly the place that they enjoyed most. It was a popular pleasure ground where, in 1786, 'several regattas, at which were present many thousands of the nobility, gentry and others from various parts were accommodated with upwards 700 sailing vessels and boats'! That description comes from the first volume of *Fen Notes and Queries*; in a later volume of this publication, skating is mentioned and immense flocks of starlings that darkened the air, alighting each evening in the reed beds. We have watched similar flocks on Tixall Wide on the Staffs & Worcs Canal and on some of the gravel pools beside the River Nene. Whittlesey Mere was drained between 1851 and 1853, the waters pumped into Bevills Leam and carried away to the sea. Other meres in the Fenland, including the one at Ramsey, have suffered the same fate.

Having enjoyed their sailing, Lord Orford's flotilla continued along the old River Nene to Stanground Sluice: 'We passed the sluice two boats at a time in five minutes each and entered Morton's Leam.' The lock was said to have a rise of 2ft and its length was only sufficient to take two boats side by side. This shows that none of their craft exceeded 49ft in length or 7ft in beam. They then continued up to Peterborough, returning later to Whittlesey Mere using Stanground Sluice, a boat at a time; the latter operation took three-quarters of an hour. Apparently the water outside was higher and it took longer to achieve the requisite level to open the gates. Even so, the boats were only taking five minutes each to pass the lock, which would therefore seem to have been in pretty good condition. On a second visit to Peterborough, the difference in level at Stanground was said to be 6ft; this difference was only to be expected as the river was still tidal at Peterborough. On their return on the second occasion, they met a 'gang of barges' at Stanground.

They later sailed to Ramsey Mere which they described as a circular lake about a mile in diameter, and then were towed by Hippopotamus for some three miles up to Ramsey. The mere was also busy with pleasure craft 'filled with both sexes . . . with angling rods in their hands'. They returned through Well Creek and Salter's Lode but had to wait until next morning to catch the tide. Again, a gang of barges was found to be waiting aground just outside the sluice. They eventually came through into the Great Ouse, passed Denver Sluice and reached home on the Lakenheath Lode after a voyage of twenty-two days.

The nineteenth century

Another early description of a pleasure cruise which, however, leaves a great deal unsaid, appears in Thomas Love Peacock's *Crotchet Castle*, published in 1831. The party made a trip in four barges, one for the men, one for the ladies, one for the servants and cooks and one for the dining room and band. These were towed by 'strong trotting horses'. They started on the Thames, passing Oxford and Lechlade and entered the Thames & Severn Canal 'ascending by many locks; passed a tunnel three miles long through the bowels of Sapperton Hill; descending many locks again through the valley of Stroud into the Severn.' There must have been so much to see but they were more interested in each other and in conversation and the record is blank. They went up the Ellesmere Canal and 'moored their pinnaces in the Vale of Llangollen by the aqueduct of Pontycyssylty'. One wonders how they reached the Ellesmere Canal for the Shroppie was uncompleted and it would have been a long way round.

Perhaps they went right up the Severn and had their boats dragged over into the Montgomeryshire Canal but they do not tell us. If only they had had someone like the Earl of Orford with them to keep a day-to-day log.

The nineteenth century was a great time for pleasure cruising, mostly on the major rivers but sometimes on the canals as well. The boats were most commonly rowed or paddled and it is not until the end of the century that powered craft appear. Thus the oarsmen or canoeists relied on finding suitable accommodation each night, which often led to their knocking up some publican at a very late hour or sleeping in most uncomfortable conditions. Tents were sometimes taken, or an awning could be stretched over bearers on some of the larger craft to make a comfortable shelter.

Several books have recently been published or reissued which throw light on the adventures of the early water travellers but rarely has the navigation itself been described in any detail. This is sad, particularly in the case of canal exploration, since so many changes have occurred that we should have liked to see things through the eyes of some of the early travellers. Few described the barges that they met, for no doubt they felt that these were a common and permanent feature that needed no description. Nevertheless, there is enough descriptive material to get a fair idea of the main rivers in the last century and of the canals in the last hundred years.

The Thames

The Thames has long been one of the main attractions to the boater and is fairly well covered in the literature. The fullest account occurs in Thacker's *The Thames Highway*, originally published in two volumes in 1914 and 1920. This work covers the river, its history, locks and flash locks, its bridges and all its features. It is, however, to the oarsmen and pleasure cruisers of bygone days that we must turn to get some idea of the actual state of the river. This is admirably summed up by the anonymous author of *The Waterway to London* (1869), who cruised from Manchester to London with two companions and a dog (shades of *Three Men in a Boat*, published twenty years later). They made the journey in a skiff and a canoe and entered the river from the Thames & Severn Canal at Lechlade. They were soon to meet the first of the flash locks and give a wonderful description of shooting it. It was a high one, probably Hart's which had a fall of up to three feet:

> Some men opened a space about five feet broad and through this the waters of the river rushed with great force and fell into the pool below. Down went the canoe . . . the stern of the boat flying up like the tail of a duck in the act of diving and reappeared floating away down the pool. I could not pull up for 30 yards or so owing to the current and then turned the canoe round to watch the progress of *Wanderer* (the skiff). I saw her bows shoot out some ten feet over the fall and then plunge down into the water . . . the next thing to be seen was the boat floating bottom upward in the pool.

Most oarsmen making a river trip sent their boat by train and then rowed downstream. I have not yet come across an account of a boat going up through a flash lock, though William Bliss described going upriver from Oxford in about 1870 (in *The Heart of England by Waterway*). He described the weirs: that at King's 'being fitted with sluice gates raised by a winch and not merely, as all others were, of paddles and rymers lifted by hand . . . There were not even rollers by the weir then and we had to go through it.' Of Hart's weir he commented: 'They have put rollers to it recently, but here is your last chance of trying your hand at lifting the paddles and rymers for yourself, as one had to do in the old days, and seeing what it is like to get up a weir that way.' Sadly, he did not tell how to pull the boat through, how long a wait was necessary or what it felt like.

The river above Oxford was in a very poor state in 1869 as is shown by the words of the anonymous author of *The*

Waterway to London: 'How to land was the question? Rushes extend in thick banks twenty feet from either shore. We could actually walk on the reeds across the river in places, although there was deep water underneath.' Below Oxford, the river was used much more fully and Jerome describes the pack of boats in Boulter's lock and the crowds at Henley during the Royal Regatta. Much has been written recently on the Thames and the well-illustrated *A Thames Companion* by Pritchard & Carpenter shows how busy it was, especially with punts and skiffs.

Many people towed their boats upstream and many more enjoyed walking the towpath for pleasure. The towpath changes sides numerous times, not always at a bridge and there were ferries at a number of places. The last of these was at Bablockhythe but even this has now been removed. There is an attractive little ferry house at Gatehampton near Goring and there are even places where the towpath is missing altogether.

An interesting sidelight on the tidal reaches through London is shown in a report by a group of gentlemen who wanted a ship canal to be built to Manchester in 1841. This noted that: 'Strollers and holiday-makers in London spend more money in the mere item of Steam Boat excursions in one summer than would pay all the clergy of the Metropolis for three years!'

The Warwickshire Avon

The Warwickshire Avon appears to come second to the Thames in popularity with the pleasure boater and many authors have written about it. The fullest descriptive account is Quiller-Couch's *The Warwickshire Avon*, illustrated by Parsons and published in 1892. They walked the upper reaches and put their Canadian canoe in the water as high upriver as Rugby, despite warnings of long shallows, three weirs, barbed wire and fallen trees. After many struggles through, round and over these obstacles, they reached

Warwick, the more common starting place for the pleasure boatman.

At Elmcote above Warwick, where the Leam joins the Avon, there were many small craft moored at the bottom of riverside gardens and they were able to leave their canoe in safety in a boathouse. Other writers have described how they had to get permission to go through the park in the grounds of Warwick castle, for the river was not officially navigable above Stratford, and much of it flowed through private land. To return to Quiller-Couch:

> We floated by flat meadows, islands of sedge, long lines of willows; by Alveston where we found boats and a boathouse covered with 'snowball' berries; by the mill and its weeping willows; and below by devious loops to Hatton Rock that picnickers from Stratford know – a steep bank of marl covered with hawthorn, hazel, elder and trailing knots of brambles.

Bliss's description of the river below Warwick brings to life the full beauties of the Avon:

> You enter Warwick Park almost at once below the bridge, lifting your canoe over and down the stone weir at its head and for a mile and a half you go through it – a mile and a half of natural beauty enhanced and not spoiled by man. The old castle stands high upon its rock at the head of the park and you should turn your head every now and then to see it looking finer and finer and gaining in dignity as you leave it behind.

He described the mills and islands between the river and the mill channel where he often camped, and how the Avon runs fast below Barford Mill with stickles and scours all the way for the next 3 miles. He considered Charlecote Park even more beautiful than Warwick Park and noted the chains across the river at each end. From there 'all the way to Stratford, the river runs fast as it did all the way to Barford and is of the same sort of scenery – the loveliest, I think, that the Avon shows.'

This type of pleasure cruising is now not possible, though it gives some idea of the attraction of the river should it ever be made navigable, as has been suggested.

Others have also made and described this cruise in books and articles and I choose only 'The Log of the *Sarah Simmons*' from *Murray's Magazine* of 1887. The writer, C. R. L. Fletcher, took his wherry from Oxford to Warwick by canal. He found that he could not get permission to row through Warwick Park so he had the boat transported to Barford and put in there. He described how the Avon differs from the upper Thames and Cherwell: 'the foliage on the bank is far grander' than on those rivers. 'It is really a very wild river; Charlecote Park is practically the one fine place we saw. The only obstructions worth mentioning were four mills between Warwick and Stratford and . . . seven between Stratford and Evesham, unless indeed the village bull at Wasperton, who made an onslaught on the passenger while the boat was being dragged over a mill, can be reckoned among obstructions'! He wondered why 'no attempt has been made to keep open the navigation, even for pleasure purposes', noting that it was navigable to Warwick and even as far as Coventry by Order of Council in James I's reign. This last statement is certainly questionable.

Below Stratford, the river was a very different proposition for it was navigable to that town until 1873 and reopened to full navigation in 1974 (pp156–8). Each of the foregoing authors described the state of the navigation as impeded by broken locks and damaged weirs (though the mill weirs were complete). The boats had to be carried round each of these obstructions and Bonthron noted in *My Holidays on Inland Waterways* (1916), that there was no towpath on any part of the Avon. He was also surprised that no charge was made for lock dues! On the Lower Avon Navigation below Evesham the nine locks were still 'in fair condition though slow to work'. Bliss commented that the first lock below Stratford was a staircase pair and described how on his visit in 1891 a little nervous for a double lock in very bad condition would be an awesome thing – we found no lock at all but only crumbling walls with the river running through them like a sluice, and a good deal of broken masonry too near the surface of the water to be pleasant. But the weir (or lasher) at the end of the other side of the island still stood, for there was a mill just below . . . We found the same state of things all the way down to Evesham and had it not been for the mills, the Avon would have been quite impossible . . .

The lock above Evesham, though it belonged to the derelict Upper Avon Navigation, had been kept in usable condition longer than the rest. From there downwards to Tewkesbury, all agree that the going was much easier and Bonthron wrote:

The motor boat has ample scope in these reaches and I found many patrolling the river, the greater number being in the lower section where there is good, available water. The attractiveness and beauties of the river were quite a revelation to us. We had, of course, heard of the Avon, but had never imagined that there were so many pleasing spots, with such plentiful foliage.

The orchards of the Vale of Evesham, the winding course of the river, the dominance of Bredon Hill rising above the lower reaches, the abbey ruins and ancient bridges are all features which most impressed the early pleasure boaters.

The Severn

Perhaps the best of several descriptions of the River Severn during the last century occurs in the anonymous *The Waterway to London*. The three men entered the Severn 15 miles above Shrewsbury and found a river so winding that they carried their craft a short distance over a hill and saved 4 miles! Their comments on a succession of rapids that hurried them along their way makes one wonder how loaded trows ever reached as far as Pool Quay. They were able to leave their boats in a boathouse at Shrewsbury since there was a fair amount of boating locally.

The description of the scenery below Shrewsbury is worth quoting: 'We enjoyed our afternoon's row down the Severn. The bold outline of the Wrekin in front, backed by the cloudless sky and receiving a rosy hue from the setting sun delighted us towards the close of the day . . . Our destination was Ironbridge; but though innumerable rapids helped us on our course, we did not reach it.' After passing Ironbridge they saw a coracle at work and tried it themselves, with poor results; they also noted the magnificent wooded scenery of Arley Park before reaching Bewdley.

Bliss paddled down the Severn in his canoe and on one occasion rowed down in a randan starting as high up as Newtown. Lengthy shallows made for slow progress in the upper reaches of the river, and even below Welshpool. However, the stretch between Welshpool and Shrewsbury delighted him:

> The Severn runs between the Breidden Hills on the right and the outposts of the distant Berwyns on the left through a valley that widens as it goes to meet the valley of the Vyrnwy. It has almost left the mountains – the Breidden Hills are the last to bar its way – and it seems to linger as if loth to leave the high lands for the low. It still runs fast but is more clothed with trees and often shut in with high banks so that for a time you see little but the overhanging trees and the water, dark in pools or dancing in rapids.

The river was full of boats at Shrewsbury, pleasure craft and school fours and eights. On Bliss's early trips there was a nasty rapid below the town 'before they built the weir', and many other rapids down as far as Bewdley. 'The country itself is perfect as it should be for it is now the country "all round the Wrekin" and that most jolly lump of a hill in England . . . will now be standing bravely on your left hand all the way to Buildwas.' He also commented on Upper Arley and the Forest of Wyre; indeed his whole description of this section makes one hope for the success of the present plans to make the river navigable by the building of locks and weirs.

Bliss and 'Anon' found the river from Stourport downwards navigable much as it is today. The former felt that the Severn had become 'a fat, comfortable river, handsome enough still, but middle aged and a little bourgeois and tending to embonpoint'! He noted that the canoe charge at the locks was threepence but the 'lashers can sometimes be shot'. The anonymous trio noted the three high weirs above Worcester, each with a lock. They carried round two of them but shot the third. Half a mile below Tewkesbury, they reached what was then the last lock on the river and decided to use it. As they were being let down, a fishing rod with a small slit in the end was pushed down to them and a man at the top gesticulated that this was for the toll. They put in two pennies and the rod was immediately withdrawn. They were then in fast-ebbing tidal waters and, as it was a spring tide, the bore was expected. Above Gloucester they pulled their boats out and the bore, 4ft high, swept up the river. There are weirs across both Partings today and, though the river is still affected by tides, the bore is very much tamed above Gloucester.

Bliss commented that the river below Worcester flows between high banks with only three bridges in 30 miles but with several ferries: 'And where there is a ferry, there is often an inn which makes companionship and keeps the river human.' At Gloucester both parties locked up into the Gloucester & Berkeley Canal.

Other river holidays
The Agecroft Rowing Club near Manchester produced a number of very fine oarsmen in the last century and their successes at regattas on the Irwell were well summed up by Corbett in *The River Irwell* (1909). The river itself is well described in the days before the Manchester Ship Canal obliterated much of its course; descriptions of weekend outings down the old navigation to Runcorn and back along the Bridgewater Canal also make good reading. As in many

nineteenth-century rowing clubs small groups of friends often took their holidays on other rivers, notably the Thames; one such group wrote up these holidays in the *Manchester City News*, the author using a pseudonym (see Bibliography).

At Whitsuntide in 1888, the group rowed the Severn from Shrewsbury to Gloucester. On this occasion they had a randan and were welcomed by the local rowing club who provided them with a cox to see them through rapids below English Bridge. After that, they were on their own and experienced considerable difficulty as the water was low, the randan was large and the party numbered seven! They thought that the scenery was at its finest between Ironbridge and Worcester and met tugs towing six or seven heavy barges below Stourport

> creating a wash and disturbance in the river which tossed us about like a cork . . . Every lock has its attendant waterfall, to mistake which is destruction. In their neighbourhood, signs 'Danger waterfall just below' but so arranged that they point to a lock as well as to the fall and you find out the latter by rowing over a constantly increasing current until a warning roar is heard and you turn back.

They noted the tidal water below Tewkesbury lock, for the tide was against them. The holiday was considered a great success but 'not to be undertaken by persons without some experience'. Today, the locks and weirs are well signposted and the waters below Tewkesbury are little affected by tides.

Four members of the group took a skiff the following August and rowed the Trent from Burton to Newark. They put their boat in the wrong channel at Burton and nearly ended up against the mill weir grill. The river takes a number of channels and one of these originally formed the navigation though the lock has long since vanished.

Once started, they found that the stream flowed strongly between flower-covered low banks and amongst herons and other water-loving birds. After Swarkeston, where they spent the night at the Crewe and Harpur Arms, 'one of the most comfortable hostelries in the county of Derby', they ran into shallows and had to drag their boat over several shoals. The only mention of the lock at King's Mills noted that 'barges could not get above Castle Donnington as the exit gate of the lock there is built up'. The remains of the lock are still visible though the lock cut is only in water below it.

From Cavendish Bridge, Shardlow they were in the navigation and had a lot of trouble with chain ferries: 'The ferries on this as on other rivers are worked by means of chains or wire ropes fixed at an altitude calculated to decapitate a crew rowing rapidly.' They noted the junction of both the Soar and the Erewash but found that in spite of the extra volume of water, the Trent shallows continued. From Nottingham to Newark they rowed without trouble, arriving in time to take part in a regatta. This length of the river was thronged with anglers though few had been seen farther upstream.

Their verdict on the Trent was that:

it is a grand river, a very paradise for boating. Though the scenery on the east side, to which lies the county of Lincoln, is flat, the rising ground of Derbyshire on the other side furnishes a perfect contrast. The rapidity of the stream reduces rowing to a pastime and fully recompenses the slight difficulties of navigation.

The locks in the lower part were said to be 'generally in good condition though cuts leading to them are almost choked with weeds'. Their final comment was, 'there is some yachting done but comparatively little boating. Save in Nottingham, we never saw "boats for hire".'

For the following two seasons, the group turned its attention to the Fen rivers, rowing the Great Ouse and Cam in August 1890 and the Nene, from Northampton to Peterborough, in May 1891. They took their skiff from Bedford but the Ouse trip was not a great success:

About half a mile after starting, there was a lock which was opened for us. On entering, a few weeds showed themselves. 'Ah, these will be over when we are out of the cutting.' But the weeds were not diminished but increased. Pushing through them at about a mile further, another lock was reached. It was broken. We didn't like it. It was rather near the town to be in that state. If such was the condition of affairs close to Bedford, what could we expect lower down. It was clear that we must carry the boat past the lock and put it in the stream below.

They described the problems of doing this, since it was difficult to get through the reeds to land the boat and as difficult to find a suitable place to relaunch it. That day they had to carry round seven more locks!

Progress was necessarily slow but the lock difficulty was a small one compared with that occasioned by the weeds, chiefly rushes. All the way till Earith was reached on Sunday, they were so thick and continuous that we scarcely ever got a reach of fifty yards of water of sufficient width to allow oars to be dipped from each side of the boat simultaneously.

The rowers were delighted with the scenery, however, and particularly with the villages whose gardens, bright with flowers, reached down to the water's edge. Beyond Earith they passed through Hermitage lock, paying a toll of 1s 6d (7½p) and were told that it used to be 2s 6d (12½p), 'but had been reduced to encourage pleasure boats'. The first 11 miles of the Old West river were so narrow that there was barely room for rowing, but it was practically weedless. Below this, and on the Cam, they found the river wider, but the high banks restricted views.

Looking back, they reflected that 'The condition of the Ouse as far as Earith is astonishing and disgraceful, it is nothing but a weed overgrown and impassable pit . . . bridged thirteen times from Bedford to Ely so near the water in many places that it looks as if the design has been formed to destroy the possibility of navigation on it.' However, they had chosen the worst time of the year for weeds and would have found the going easier in the spring.

It was in late May 1891 that the group attempted the Nene, starting from Northampton where there were rollers to help them past the first lock. Despite the time of year, snow was falling when they reached Wellingborough. The very numerous locks were all in working order and the channel was good; the locks themselves were not those that we know today but ones built in the early nineteenth century. The stretch near Lilford Hall was described as 'one of the most beautiful spots on the river' and this is indeed still the case. A lot of barge traffic was noted below Oundle including a hold-up at Wansford lock to allow barges to be taken through. At Milton Park, above Peterborough, they followed a train of four such craft pulled by one horse. Nearby staunches remained in place since they held up sufficient water for the barges and could not be opened for the group's boat, which had to be dragged out and carried round.

The Nene valley was 'a continuous scene of pastoral beauty varied and relieved by woods and innumerable slopes'. The rarity of pleasure boats on the river was emphasised by the fact that at some villages 'our coming was made known in advance'. The river itself was sometimes narrow and often winding and the towpath was in good order. The railway was never far away, which they found most useful since they could leave the boat in a safe place and take the train back to Wellingborough for the night. This is now not possible, though the attractive private Nene Valley Railway lies by the lower reaches.

Canal journeys
Several accounts exist of canal cruises in the last decades of the nineteenth century and in the early days of this. In many cases, however, the writer was keener to describe his adventures than to give any details of the waterways as he found them.

191

One of the most complete descriptions is contained in John Hollingshead's oft-quoted 'On the Canal' published in *Household Words* in 1858, and republished in 1973 by the Waterways Museum at Stoke Bruerne. Hollingshead was a passenger on the fly boat *Stourport* from London through to Birmingham. The importance to us of his trip lies in the fact that he described the boat and its bright paintings (the first recorded full description), the boaters and their ways, including their meals, and a boaters' village which had the pub, grocer and tailor all housed in one building.

The inside of the living cabin, which was kept spotless, is described in great detail and clearly differed little from the typical butty cabin that we know today. His inaccurate dimensions for the boat leave much to be desired but otherwise the descriptions appear to be accurate. The fly boat travelled by night as well as by day and the horses 'are as docile, intelligent and well-behaved as the trained steeds at a circus; and, for many miles, they are left to go unled'. There is a good description of legging and of boats passing one another in a tunnel; the locks are also well portrayed and the eerie feelings of locking through at night.

There is some evocation of the actual countryside with its 'rich grass banks', the patient anglers on the towpath and the 'distant red-bricked mansions' with 'smooth-shaved lawns' and 'parks and gardens running down to the water's edge'. The entry to Birmingham alongside 'coal heaps and white roaring mouths of furnaces, past myriad-windowed factories whose glass is broken' gives a poor impression of the Black Country. A little of this may still be seen but most of it has been cleared up and the Birmingham Canal Navigations are much more pleasant today.

For me, the finest descriptions of late nineteenth-century canals are those given by Bliss, though his book was not published until 1933. Amongst the canals he cruised were the Oxford, the Napton & Warwick (now part of the Grand Union), the Gloucester & Berkeley, the Stroudwater, and the

192

Thames & Severn Canals. His account of camping in the Golden Valley near the Daneway entrance to Sapperton tunnel is one of the best pieces of descriptive prose that I have ever read. I reread it often and read it aloud in lectures on that canal. It is too long to quote in full but he tells of the moonlight slanting through the trees and lighting up patches of sweet-smelling butterfly-orchis. As he stood entranced, a nightingale burst into song: 'Nowhere else in the world but on an English river or canal could such beauty of night and scent and sound have been mine.' It is still a lovely valley and one can only hope that the volunteer society will succeed in reopening it to full navigation.

There is a fine description of passing through Wast Hill tunnel on the Worcester & Birmingham Canal in William Black's novel *The Strange Adventures of a House Boat*. A biography of the author shows that he made his canal trip, though his actual boat was somewhat less palatial than that described in the book. They were waiting with other boats near the entrance to the tunnel when there

appeared a black and grimy little steam launch; . . . we were furnished with a lamp to be fixed on the bow; and thereupon, the burly little steamer proceeded to head the long line. How the line was formed, it was hard to say; but it was clear that we were to be at the tail-end of it; and indeed, as barge after barge moved away, we had no more than time to throw a rope to the last of them and get attached. The huge black snake before us was disappearing into the bowels of the earth with a marvellous rapidity; one had to steer as straight as one could for the small narrow arch at the base of the mighty mass of masonry; the semicircular opening seemed to close around us; and the next moment we were in darkness.

We only knew there was a wall around us for we grated along this side and then banged against that; and altogether the situation was unpleasant. But matters mended a little. Whether the smoke from the launch had lessened or not, one could at length make out two dull spots of orange, doubtless two lamps and these at least gave some indication of our course, and some guidance for steering. The worst of it was that this light boat at the end of these heavy barges would not properly answer her helm; and the swing they gave her was too powerful.

Suddenly into the hollow-sounding vault there springs a shrill high plaintive note; and we find that one of the younger bargemen has begun to relieve the tedium of this subterranean passage with a pathetic ballad. So silent was the tunnel – for there is only the dull throbbing far away of the engine of the steam launch – that every word can be distinctly heard.

They were in the tunnel for three-quarters of an hour and were delighted at last to see a sort of miniature bullseye of a dullish hue, that disappeared now and then behind clouds of smoke;

but ever as we glided or grated along, it was growing larger and larger . . . And now we could make out an archway filled with a suffused yellow light; the black barges are sailing towards it and through it . . . finally – with eyes dazed with the sudden splendour of colour – we sail out into the placid beauty of this bit of Worcestershire scenery – green wooded banks and brown water, and the overhanging trees all warm in the light of the afternoon sky.

In the present century, the steam tug was replaced by one driven by a petrol/paraffin and later a diesel engine; one such craft, the tug *Worcester*, is a prized possession of the Boat Museum.

C. J. Aubertin, writing in 1916, described how he came to Harecastle tunnel, which then had an electric tug: 'It pulls twenty barges and therefore (having paid 6d for the privilege) we aligned ourselves twentieth on the string and prepared for the Cimmerian gloom ahead.' Unfortunately for them, the tunnel-keeper decided that their boat was too high and they had to bowhaul it instead. Even at that date, the tunnel had subsided and the towpath had vanished beneath the surface of the water so that the one towing was knee-deep in water.

Coming nearer to the present day, we have in *Narrow Boat* Rolt's beautiful descriptions of many of the canals as he saw them just before the last war. When he cruised them they had changed little for over a century. During the war, a number of women trained to take over the jobs of boatmen on active service and, for a spell, they became boat people themselves. Three of them – Susan Woolfitt, Emma Smith and Eily Gayford – wrote books (see Bibliography) to tell of their experiences; Tim Wilkinson and his wife did much the same. Their books tell us something of the lives and the thoughts of the traditional boaters and describe the waterways in all their moods, both in summer and in winter. They tell of a community that has practically disappeared in our lifetime and of canals being used for the purpose for which they were built.

USEFUL ADDRESSES

For those who want to know more of canals and to meet others interested, there are many avenues open. Perhaps the first thing to do is to join the Inland Waterways Association (114 Regent's Park Road, London NW1 8UQ). It has local branches, each of which organises winter meetings and a number of other activities. The cruising fraternity can be met at cruising clubs and the fishermen at angling associations; the names and addresses of the secretaries can be found in the British Waterways Board's annual *Waterway User's Companion* (obtainable direct from the Board's offices at Melbury House, Melbury Terrace, London NW1 6JX). Many people want to be more active in restoring canals and they should join the Waterway Recovery Group (via Alan Jervis, 39 Westminster Crescent, Burn Bridge, Harrogate HG3 1LX); its bimonthly magazine *Navvies* gives details of all volunteer work taking place. There are also the regular waterways magazines: *Waterways World* and *Canal and River Boat*, both of which appear monthly and may be ordered from the local newsagent. In addition, the British Waterways Board publishes *Waterways News* which may be obtained direct by subscription.

There are certain waterways museums that should be visited. Prime amongst these is the National Waterways Museum, usually known as the Boat Museum, Dockyard Road, Ellesmere Port, South Wirral. The British Waterways Board has established an attractive museum, the Waterways Museum, in a canalside warehouse at Stoke Bruerne, Towcester, Northampton, on the Grand Union Canal. It also proposes to start another in the Gloucester dock complex. The Black Country Museum, Tipton Road, Dudley, includes a length of canal with a boat-builder's yard and a number of boats; the Ironbridge Gorge Museum, Ironbridge, Telford, Shropshire, has a tub-boat canal and the restored Hay inclined plane. The Canal Exhibition Centre, The Wharf, Llangollen, Clwyd, and the museum in the Clock Warehouse (Plus Pleasure Marine) at Shardlow, near Derby, both tell the story of canal building and use, whilst the Canal Museum, Canal Street, Nottingham, concentrates on the carriers Fellows, Morton & Clayton.

The National Maritime Museum, Romney Road, Greenwich, London, the Exeter Maritime Museum, The Quay, Exeter, and the Mersey Maritime Museum, The Pierhead, Liverpool, are mostly devoted to sea-going craft, ship-building and trade but each has some exhibits from the inland waterways. All are certainly worth lengthy visits. The attractive Steamboat Museum, Bayrigg Road, Windermere, has beautifully restored lakeland craft and many other museums in the country have sections on inland waterways.

BIBLIOGRAPHY

For those who really want to study the history of our canal and river navigations, volumes in the *Canals of the British Isles* series, many written by Charles Hadfield, are available from bookshops and libraries and from the publishers, David & Charles of Newton Abbot, Devon. Several of them are specifically referred to below.

Anon. *The Waterway to London* (John Heywood, 1869)

Aubertin, C. J. *A Caravan Afloat* (Simpkin, Marshall, Hamilton Kent & Co, *c*1916)

Black, W. *The Strange Adventures of a House Boat* (Sampson Low, Marston, Searle & Rivington, 1888)

Bliss, W. *The Heart of England by Waterway* (H. F. & G. Witherby, 1933)

Blunt, R. 'On Tow' *Pall Mall* magazine (1888; reprinted IWA Bulletin, October 1966)

Bonthron, P. *My Holidays on Inland Waterways* (Thomas Murby, 1916)

British Waterways Board. *The Waterway User's Companion* (London, annually)

Childers, A. W. (ed) *Lord Orford's Voyage round the Fens* (Cantley, 1868)

Corbett, J. *The River Irwell* (Abel Heywood, 1907)

Fletcher, C. R. L. 'The Log of the *Sarah Simmons*', *Murray's Magazine*, Vol II (1887)

Gayford, E. *The Amateur Boatwomen* (David & Charles, 1973)

Hadfield, C. *British Canals*, 7th edn (David & Charles, 1984)

——, —. *The Canals of South West England*, 2nd edn (David & Charles, 1985)

——, —. *The Canals of the East Midlands* (David & Charles, 1970)

——, —. *The Canals of the West Midlands*, 2nd edn (David & Charles, 1985)

——, —. & Biddle, G. *The Canals of North West England*, Vols I & II (David & Charles, 1970)

199

Bibliography

——, —. & Skempton, A. W. *William Jessop, Engineer* (David & Charles, 1979)

Hanson, H. *The Canal Boatmen, 1760–1914* (Manchester University Press, 1973)

Hollingshead, J. 'On the Canal', *Household Words* (1858; reprinted Waterways Museum, 1973)

Jerome, J. K. *Three Men in a Boat* (Penguin, 1967)

Langford, J. I. *Staffordshire & Worcestershire Canal* Towpath Guide No 1 (Goose & Son, 1974)

Lewery, A. J. *Narrow Boat Painting* (David & Charles, 1974)

Malet, H. *Bridgewater: the Canal Duke, 1736–1803* (Manchester University Press, 1977)

Mather, F. C. *After the Canal Duke* (Clarendon Press, 1970)

McKnight, H. *The Shell Book of Inland Waterways*, 2nd edn (David & Charles, 1981)

Owen, D. E. *Water Rallies* (Dent, 1969)

——, —. *The Manchester Ship Canal* (Manchester University Press, 1983)

Peacock, T. L. *Crotchet Castle* (London, 1831; Penguin, 1969)

Pollins, H. *Britain's Railways* (David & Charles, 1971)

Prior, M. *Fisher Row* (Clarendon Press, 1982)

Pritchard, M. & Carpenter, H. *A Thames Companion* (Clarendon Press, 1981)

Quiller-Couch, A. T. *The Warwickshire Avon* (London, 1892)

Ransom, P. J. G. *The Archaeology of Canals* (Worlds Work, 1979)

Rolt, L. T. C. *Narrow Boat* (Eyre & Spottiswoode, 1944)

——, —. *The Inland Waterways of England* (George Allen & Unwin, 1950)

——, —. *Thomas Telford* (Longmans, 1958)

Russell, R. *Lost Canals and Waterways of Britain* (David & Charles, 1982)

Smith, E. *Maidens Trip* (MacGibbon & Kee, 1948)

Thacker, F. S. *The Thames Highway: Vol I, General History* (London, 1914; David & Charles, 1968)

——, —. *The Thames Highway: Vol II, Locks & Weirs* (London, 1920; David & Charles, 1968)

Warrington, J. (ed) *The Diary of Samuel Pepys* (Everyman, 1953)

Wilkinson, T. *Hold on a Minute* (George Allen & Unwin, 1965)

Woolfitt, S. *Idle Women* (Ernest Benn, 1947)

Young, A. *Six Months Tour through the North of England* (London, 1771)

Fen Notes and Queries (Vol I, 1889–90; Vol V, 1901–03)

Bibliography

Manchester City News (9 June, 1888; 24 & 31 August, 1889; 16 August, 1890; 30 May, 1891)

Oarsman's and Angler's Map of the River Thames, The (London, 1884)

Ship Canal News (Manchester, 1887–94)

ACKNOWLEDGEMENTS

The author wishes to thank Mr Alan Warhurst, Director of Manchester Museum and Mr Wilf Thomas, museum photographer, for printing the photographs from the author's collection. His thanks are also due to Mr Charles Hadfield for reading and suggesting improvements to the manuscript. He thanks Mr Keith Robinson for drawing the map.

He is also grateful to his wife, Pearl, for her encouragement and for steering through all locks, however dark and deep.

INDEX

Figures in *italic* indicate main entry

Index